E-Business Best Practices

E-Business Best Practices

LEVERAGING TECHNOLOGY FOR BUSINESS ADVANTAGE

Stewart McKie

John Wiley & Sons, Inc.
New York • Chichester • Weinheim • Brisbane • Singapore • Toronto

This book is printed on acid-free paper. ∞

Published simultaneously in Canada.

Library of Congress Cataloging-in-Publication Data:

McKie, Stewart.
E-business best practices : leveraging technology for business advantage / Stewart McKie.
p. cm.
Includes bibliographical references and index.
ISBN 0-471-40251-6 (cloth : alk. paper)
1. Business enterprises—Computer networks. 2. Management.
3. Electronic commerce.
I. Title.
HD30.37.M393 2001
658.8'4—dc21 00-068543

Printed in the United States of America.

10 9 8 7 6 5 4 3 2 1

ABOUT THE AUTHOR

Stewart McKie is an independent consultant and technology writer specializing in business management software. He is the author of four books on business management software and some 200 articles, many on e-business topics, for magazines such as *Business Finance, Intelligent Enterprise, Computers in Finance,* and others. Mr. McKie has worked with many North American and European end user corporations and software vendors. He can be reached via his Web site at www.cfoinfo.com.

To my wife Theresa

ACKNOWLEDGMENTS

The author would like to acknowledge some individuals who have enhanced, recognized, or supported his own e-business perspectives, including David Blansfield as publisher of *Business Finance* magazine, Justin Kestelyn as editor of *Intelligent Enterprise* magazine, Mike Rohan as president of FRx Software, and Torben Wind as vice president of Product Development at Navision Software.

CONTENTS

PREFACE

WHO SHOULD READ THIS BOOK?

This book is for business managers, software consultants and resellers, and business or technology students who want an introduction to e-business best practices from a software perspective. It is not targeted at information technology (IT) people specifically or at business managers looking to find best practice implementation plans for use in a specific business context.

If you are interested in e-business issues and trends from a technology perspective; in the new generation of business management software; in better process automation; and in ideas for how to bring software-driven best practices to your organization, then this book is for you.

WHAT IS THIS BOOK ABOUT?

This book is about leveraging technology and, in particular, software technology to help implement e-business best practices in an organization. The book focuses on 10 e-business best practice topics and makes dozens of suggestions—boxed in the text as Best Practice Action tips—for taking practical steps to reach best practice. The aim is to provide enough background and ideas on each topic to encourage readers to initiate their own e-business best practice initiatives in their organizations or those of their clients.

WHAT IS E-BUSINESS?

The term "E-business" can describe both a type of business and a way of doing business. As a type of business, an e-business is generally accepted to be a company focused on delivering products and/or services via the Internet—a so-called dot-com company. As a way of doing business, e-business refers to the use of business processes that leverage technology—and especially the Internet and World Wide Web (the Web)—to maintain or create competitive advantage. This book is not about dot-com companies but is about ways of doing business.

In any case, soon every company will either be, or at least partly operate as, a dot-com company—it will have to do so in order to leverage new best practice processes that depend on the Internet and the Web. But before e-business becomes business as usual—which seems likely to happen in the current decade (2000–2010)—there is a transition phase to go through. During this phase business models are constantly morphing, business processes are in a state of flux, and best practices are being redefined. This book aims to help readers understand some key aspects of this transition phase and take actions to enable them to survive in good shape.

You can practice e-business without using the Internet, Web, or other emerging technologies such as extensible markup language (XML). But you will need to make active use of all three to achieve e-business best practice, using the technologies discussed in this book. E-business uses technology to automate and continuously improve business processes to make them faster, cheaper, and better and to allow human resources to focus on more value-added business tasks.

WHAT ARE BEST PRACTICES?

In a strict sense, best practice is what an industry leader has achieved and represents a benchmark for other businesses to aim for. Or put another way, as defined by the Best Manufacturing Practices organization: "A Best Practice is a process, technique, or innovative use of equipment or resources that has a proven record of success in providing significant improvement in cost, schedule, quality, performance, safety, environment or other measurable factors which impact the health of an organization." (See www.bmpcoe.org/faq/index.html.)

Best practice does not necessarily depend on the use of technology. But the use of technology is becoming more and more influential in helping firms to reach best practice levels of operational efficiency, especially as software technology is applied to the automation of more and more business processes.

This book takes a more liberal view of best practices by discussing and recommending initiatives that will help businesses achieve best practice, rather than attempting to define *the* best practice for a given e-business situation. Because best practices never stand still, especially in a rapidly developing area such as e-business, the book does not aim to prescribe what best practices are for specific businesses or business situations. Instead it aims to provide a framework for creating and implementing your own best practices by leveraging the concepts and technologies discussed herein.

DISCLAIMERS

This book does not:

- Review specific software products, make product recommendations, or provide how-to-operate instructions for software packages.
- Make extensive use of detailed case study material, since plenty of best practice case studies can be found in many of the works listed in the Selected Readings resource section.
- Make extensive use of industry analyst opinions or research, it is assumed that many readers will work for corporations that subscribe to these analyst services already.

This book does:

- Highlight specific vendors or software products by name as examples of well-known or innovative market players or application packages.
- Make use of material from some 200 articles I wrote for *Business Finance* and *Intelligent Enterprise* magazines between 1995 and 2000.
- Make use of data from the *Book of Numbers* published annually by benchmarking specialists, Hackett Benchmarking

Solutions (part of the AnswerThink Consulting Group). While I have no connection with Hackett, I believe their research is useful and regularly updated.

OUTLINE OF BOOK CHAPTERS

Introduction

The introduction outlines some key attributes that are needed by the individual business transformers who are charged with leading e-business initiatives and discusses the concept of business asset management.

1. E-Business Landscape

The technology landscape is changing all the time. This chapter outlines a number of foundation technologies that every e-business will depend on.

2. E-Business Management: Going Beyond ERP

Enterprise resource planning (ERP) was a technology success story of the 1990s. This chapter discusses how organizations are finding it necessary to move beyond traditional ERP applications and embrace a broader vision of business management software.

3. Monitor to Manage: Enterprise Positioning System

Every enterprise needs its own version of a global positioning system (GPS) in the form of an enterprise positioning system (EPS). This chapter discusses the tools and techniques needed to track and monitor the many transaction systems a typical e-business operates.

4. Collaborate to Compete

The Internet and the Web provide an infrastructure for effective and efficient collaboration. This chapter discusses business-to-consumer (B2C) and business-to-business (B2B) supply chain collaboration and the importance of new online trading hubs.

5. Customer Relationship Management

Customer relationships are increasingly being managed electronically. This chapter discusses how to acquire, retain, and leverage the new generation of e-customers using various types of customer relationship management (CRM) software.

6. E-Procurement

Every e-business wants to keep costs low. E-procurement practice and technology helps businesses take advantage of new ways to source suppliers and products and move closer to paperless purchasing.

7. Knowledge Management

Knowledge can be one of the most disorganized and underutilized business assets. This chapter discusses how knowledge management can be used to take advantage of the knowledge assets hidden in every organization.

8. Digital Asset Management

E-businesses need to practice effective digital asset management, since digital assets represent some of the most valuable assets they own. This chapter discusses ways to better manage digital assets such as Web sites, documents, and messages.

9. Software as Service

Application and business service providers (ASPs and BSPs) now offer an alternative to the traditional software build-or-buy decision. This chapter discusses application outsourcing and Web-based service providing, both of which are helping to convert shrink-wrapped software into Web services delivered over the Internet.

10. XML Everywhere

Extensible markup language (XML) is set to become a critical e-business technology. This chapter introduces XML and outlines some of the ways that it can be used to reengineer business processes.

11. Hackett Benchmarking Solutions on Best Practices

The Hackett Group pioneered independent benchmarking research and best practice definition. This chapter summarizes the latest research from the year 2000 edition of the annual *The Book of Numbers* publication.

Selected Readings and Glossary

This section lists where to find more information about e-business and best practices through books, magazines, and Web sites plus a short glossary of terms used in the text.

Introduction

The premise of this book is that to become an e-business, an organization has to leverage technology. And to maintain or gain competitive edge from taking advantage of technology, managers need to aim for best practice utilization. A significant problem in achieving best practice utilization of technology is that the rapid pace of technology change is making best practice implementation a moving target. That is why those who practice e-business must have both a sense of urgency and plenty of attitude.

For businesses making the transition to e-business, time is of the essence. Online commerce pioneers often reckon that a year is the equivalent to a month in so-called Internet time. A flood of venture capital attracted by the promise of stellar gains has created a vigorous gene pool of dot-com companies all vying to achieve first-mover advantage in new or emerging e-business markets. New entrants, acquisitions, and strategic partnerships happen on a daily basis, sometimes changing the profile of a marketplace overnight. E-business and dot-com company stocks are subject to volatile swings in demand and valuation as someone or something becomes the flavor of the month and is hyped up by the business media. Time is of the essence because e-business is at the land-rush stage of development where there is plenty of territory to carve out and many choice plots to settle on.

But a sense of urgency is only one of many attributes an e-business needs to adopt; any business aiming to be an e-business also needs plenty of attitude. By attitude I mean a mind-set shared by the executives, managers, and employees charged with effecting business transformation. Only people with the right e-business attitude can become the transformers needed to push through the cultural, technology, business model, and process changes required to create e-businesses.

An e-business transformer

- Tries to think from the outside-in, like a customer
- Accepts technology churn as just the way it is
- Practices business asset management
- Operates as a process demolition expert

If individuals or, better still, whole organizations can adopt this transformer attitude, the road to e-business is likely to be a lot easier.

BEST PRACTICE ACTION ► DEVELOP AN E-BUSINESS ATTITUDE. Encourage a customer-focused culture based on better understanding of customer behavior. Look at your technology churn rates to determine if you are holding on to some technology too long or getting the expected return from your investments. Identify your key business assets and construct an ideal asset profile from which to assess the worth of your current asset portfolio and plan future acquisitions. Regularly evaluate every business process to make sure no one thinks that any process is protected from change.

THINKING OUTSIDE-IN

Until recently, many businesses have largely paid lip service to the idea of responding to customer needs. For example, market research and focus groups, while useful for gaining valuable feedback from prospective and existing customers, do little to help create stronger customer relationships.

Thinking outside-in involves a significant cultural change for many businesses. Today's customers are becoming more demanding in their expectations and more fickle in their loyalties. When the corner store lost out to the mall, customers swapped the advantage of convenience for the benefits of lower prices, longer opening times, and a more varied shopping experience. The same transition is being made today as businesses and consumers are being offered the opportunity to shop at a vast selection of online markets and malls. Competition for the customer is no longer constrained by geographic and time-related boundaries: A customer with an Internet connection can now be serviced from anywhere, at any time. That is why getting closer to customers and understanding their behavior in order to deliver products and services that truly meet the needs of selected demand niches is a vital skill for business transformers to develop.

Getting closer to customers means catalyzing cultural change within your organization by implementing technology that makes it easier to interact with customers, monitor customer behavior, and respond to customer demands. This technology could include customer relationship management (CRM) software, Web site clickstream analysis software, and lean-manufacturing systems. Exploiting this technology should mean that businesses can identify customer product and service solutions faster and deliver them more rapidly in customized one-to-one formats for optimum customer satisfaction.

BEST PRACTICE ACTION ► CREATE A CUSTOMER CULTURE. Creating a customer culture is not just about getting closer to external business or consumer customers. It is also about getting internal departments to implement their own customer culture by identifying who their customers are and what service or product they are delivering. For example, does your finance department know who its customers are, what services it should be delivering to them, and whether those services are meeting customer needs?

TECHNOLOGY CHURN

Technology churn is the process of continually replacing technology assets to reflect the need to respond to advances in hardware and software capabilities. Every e-business is likely to operate with a mixed bag of technologies, applications, and perhaps even user interfaces as a result of ongoing technology churn.

Technology churn is not being triggered by an information technology (IT) department's desire to play with new toys or learn new skills for resume enhancement—activities that have no place in an e-business. Technology churn supports a basic business principle: Adapt to survive. Accepting the need for technology churn means accepting that technology assets will have shorter life cycles than anticipated by traditional return on investment (ROI) expectations. Any technology that takes years to implement, as some ERP systems have proven to take, is unlikely to deliver the best ROI since the original technology probably will be overtaken by better, faster, cheaper technology in the meantime.

In an e-business, the term "legacy systems"—typically referring to the minicomputer and mainframe-based systems still running many of the world's largest corporations—is now obsolete. A legacy is a one-time event, an inheritance that is gradually spent or worn out. A better term is heritage systems, because by the time a system is delivering on its ROI expectations, it may already be a legacy system in the fast-moving world of e-business technology.

E-business managers have to accept the fact that due to technology churn, more and more systems within a business are becoming part of the heritage systems. This new reality creates a need for new technology and new business skills. For example, new technology is required to support business-to-business application integration that goes beyond the enterprise application integration (EAI) technology designed to facilitate application-to-application connection. And new business skills are required to plan the technology succession strategies that smooth out the potentially disruptive impact of technology churn.

Regular technology audits, preferably overseen by the chief executive or chief financial officer, are necessary both to stimulate technology churn and to avoid excessive technology churn. These audits should attempt to review current technology assets to identify technology

- That needs churning in order to deliver better value to the business

- That better supports businesses processes subject to process demolition
- Is operating at well above or well below anticipated ROI expectations

The expectation of higher levels of technology churn is another reason why the opportunity to outsource more enterprise applications is looking more attractive every day. Technology churn puts a strain on IT infrastructures and the people who maintain them. Outsourcing the technology churn burden to an application service provider (ASP) is one way to reduce the strain and focus on the core competencies of the business.

BEST PRACTICE ACTION ➤ LEARN TO CHURN. Try to control technology churn through the use of regular technology audits designed to highlight and plan for potential future churn candidates. Always apply the maxim "Build, Buy, or Broker" when deciding how to go about replacing a current application that may no longer meet its functional or ROI expectations.

BUSINESS ASSET MANAGEMENT

Business asset management depends on a business model change that is focused on the assets of the business rather than its functions. To implement business asset management means first understanding what your business assets are and then taking the necessary steps to acquire, retain, and leverage those assets as effectively as possible. For the service-focused, collaborative corporations of the future, more efficient management of the people, partner, process and other nonmaterial or intangible assets of the business is likely to pay far bigger dividends than traditional fixed asset management.

Business assets are those entities that support the achievement of business goals. If you ask a drill sergeant the purpose of an infantryman, the answer will almost invariably be "to kill the enemy." The drill sergeant views the infantryman as a battle asset who is used to reach a very specific goal and who is organized in battle formations designed to optimally achieve that goal.

Unlike the military, businesses tend not to be organized around the achievement of specific asset-driven business goals. Instead, they focus their efforts and organize them around functions or departments, such as accounting or sales. It is argued that this focus will not work for e-businesses, because the pace of innovation and the level of competition forces them to become goal-focused organizations that depend on effective and efficient business asset management as a better way to achieve business goals. Business asset management treats specific business entities as assets and looks at ways to better manage those assets in order to reach business goals faster, cheaper, and more effectively.

A typical e-business will have at least five key business assets:

1. People
2. Partners
3. Processes
4. Knowledge
5. Technology

In fact, the one asset type that e-businesses are least likely to consider strategic is the traditional fixed asset in the form of buildings, fixtures, and fittings. The increasing numbers of road warriors and home-office workers, the decreasing numbers of clerical and middle management workers, and more flexible equipment and service leasing arrangements are making the need for accumulating fixed assets less critical. Corporate locations are becoming less of a workplace and more like a car dealer showroom where meetings are arranged, products and services are discussed and demonstrated, and basic back-office (accounting, etc.) "repair work" is carried out.

Some organizations have realized that even their heritage fixed assets can be leveraged in different ways to take advantage of new business opportunities. For example, the United Kingdom gas utility provider Transco is laying fiber-optic telecom lines alongside its gas pipelines and converting its network of internal communications towers into base stations for mobile phone operators. Also in the United Kingdom, the milk-delivery company Unigate expects to utilize its fleets of vehicles to provide the delivery capability for online shopping services that deliver food direct to the door. These are just two examples of the type of innovative business asset management practice required of e-business transformers.

Switching to an asset management focus demands its own change of attitude for e-business managers. Organization charts may require dramatic reorganization so that vice president—(VP) or director-level jobs are created for top-level asset manager positions. A new VP of Customers may work alongside the VP of Sales, or a new chief knowledge officer (CKO) may work alongside the CFO.

These new positions reflect the fact that asset management has a different focus from functional management. For example, the VP of Customers may be primarily concerned with how the business acquires, retains, and leverages customers—something that may not, in practice, be high on the agenda of a function-based VP of Sales or Marketing. Managing these assets effectively depends on using asset management systems that let managers pinpoint what and where their assets are and monitor how they are performing. Many of today's businesses still do not have in place work-flow or knowledge management systems that enable managers to manage organizational process or knowledge assets.

> **BEST PRACTICE ACTION** ► **FLAUNT YOUR ASSETS.** Once you have identified what your business assets are, make sure your business stakeholders know that you care about them. Highlight skilled employees on the corporate intranet, publicize your patents and technology successes, reward business partners for best performance criteria, and benchmark your processes against the competition wherever possible.

PROCESS DEMOLITION

Process demolition is a little more radical than the business process reengineering (BPR) initiatives that were advocated in the late 1980s and early 1990s. Here, the business transformer is not concerned with incremental change to existing processes but with the proposition and implementation of wholly new processes that take best advantage of a raft of new technology. In practice, these new processes may demand incremental implementation, but an e-business attitude starts with a clean-sheet approach and works forward, integrating existing process steps where appropriate and rejecting them when they are not.

To understand more clearly what is meant by process demolition from an e-business perspective, let us examine how it could be applied to a common business process such as procurement, the business-to-business buying process.

In most businesses, there are at least two types of procurement:

1. Buying goods and services used as an integral part of the delivery of goods and services to a customer
2. Buying goods and services used in the operations of the business that support the delivery of goods and services to a customer

I will refer to type one as delivery procurement and type two as operational procurement and focus on the operational procurement process.

Exhibit I.1 outlines a traditional operational procurement process. Even with a relatively modern procurement system in place, this process is cumbersome. Although much of the paper inherent in the process has been removed, it has been replaced with on-screen forms, electronic data interchange (EDI) transactions, and approval via electronic in boxes.

Faced with this scenario, a process demolition expert might ask the following questions:

- Why is a requisition being created at all? If operational resources are properly inventoried, then an inventory issue from the ERP system could have automatically triggered the dispatch of a requisition to the supplier to replenish the inventory (subject to economic order quantities, etc.). Automatic requisition generation is based on business rules linked to this inventory item that demand a response to the event of an item hitting its reorder quantity.
- Why does the requisition need to be passed to an internal purchasing department? If preferred supplier procurement is

Exhibit I.1 A Traditional Operational Procurement Process

Step	*Description*
1. Create Requisition	Employee creates requisition for operational resource.
2. Approve Requisition	Manager approves/disapproves requisition.
3. Process Requisition	Requisition is passed to the purchasing department for conversion or consolidation into an official order.
4. Submit Order	A purchase order is submitted to the supplier.
5. Order Confirmed	The supplier sends an order confirmation detailing any exceptions to the order if appropriate.
6. Receive Goods	The goods are received at a receiving bay and the receipt confirmed in the system by the receiving party.
7. Route Goods	The goods are delivered to the requisitioner who confirms that goods are fit for their purpose.
8. Receive Invoice	The invoice is received and matched against what was ordered and what was received (three-way match).
9. Approve Invoice	The invoice is approved for payment.
10. Pay Invoice	A payment is processed to the supplier to settle the invoice.

being practiced, the requisition can be transmitted automatically and electronically directly to the supplier over the Internet. If best-price procurement is being practiced, the requisition can be submitted electronically to online marketplaces to effect a reverse-auction, request-for-bid process or participate in group-buying. In the pre-Internet world, time constraints prevented the in-house purchasing from attempting to get bids for each requisition.

- Why does the requisition need approval? Server-based workflow business rules should exist that minimize need for managerial approval of an operational procurement requisition unless a defined exception condition occurs.

- Why is there any need for an invoice receipt and a three-way match? If the goods received are what were requested, payment can be generated automatically and transmitted electronically without waiting for an invoice, assuming the supplier's details are already stored in the system.

These and other questions show how testing the fundamental assumptions of a process results in process demolition. Looking for opportunities to use new technology to speed up or collapse a typical process can effectively "demolish" even a well-established business process.

BEST PRACTICE ACTION ► **INTERNET TEST EVERY STEP.** When evaluating business processes for change, examine each process step and ask the question: How can I leverage the Internet and Web for this step? The answer may not always be practicable at this time but it is likely to expand the possibilities for the process step execution and create a useful wish list for use in future process improvement initiatives.

The journey toward e-business best practices starts with a sense of urgency and an attitude that thinks outside-in, embraces technology churn, practices asset management, and treats no business process as sacred. In the next chapter, we will look at the e-business landscape from the perspective of a business transformer looking for opportunities for change.

CHAPTER ONE

E-Business Landscape

If one feature can be said to dominate the e-business landscape, it has to be the Internet. The Internet and the Web have triggered a number of changes in business models and processes, technology architectures, and the way that application software in particular is designed, deployed, and used.

The e-business landscape changes all the time, but as of mid-2000 some of its other more important features include

- **Browser/Server.** The terminal/host and client/server architectures of the past are being merged into the Internet-based information management architecture of the future.
- **Clickstream Farming.** As more and more interactions with businesses are conducted online, it has become vital to capture and analyze user clickstreams to more clearly understand their behavior and needs.
- **Document-level APIs.** By codifying documents using XML, every document will have its own API to make all kinds of corporate information easier to access and analyze programmatically.
- **Event-Aware Enterprises.** Downsizing and lean staffing means that businesses must trap and action exceptional business events with minimum human oversight.
- **Everything's a URL.** IP addresses on the Internet will make anything, anywhere addressing a reality.

- **Four Faces of the Internet.** Every business will need to create four faces, two private and two public, to represent itself over the Internet.
- **Integration Rules.** A batch-driven application integration architecture will not cut it in the world of e-business.
- **ISP to ASP to BSP.** Internet service providing options are getting more sophisticated all the time as ISPs are joined by ASPs and BSPs.
- **Matchmaking.** One-to-one B2B commerce models have been expanded to include one-to-many and many-to-many models.
- **Portals on the World.** Accessing the vast range of information and services accessible over the Internet demands new ways of organizing these resources efficiently.

The e-business landscape can be compared to the formative years of the earth's early geological periods. Volcanoes and earthquakes dominate today's e-business landscape rather than the gradual, long-term processes of erosion or climate change.

The following acronyms are used in this chapter

TERM	DESCRIPTION
API	Application programming interface
ASP	Application service provider
B2B	Business to business
BSP	Business service provider
EAI	Enterprise application integration
IP	Internet protocol
ISP	Internet service provider
URL	Uniform resource locator
VDU	Visual display unit

BROWSER/SERVER

In the first few decades of business computing we have witnessed a migration from centralized terminal/host architectures to distributed client/server architectures. In the year 2000, the next evolution of computing architectures, the move to browser/server architecture, is in full swing. (See Exhibit 1.1 for comparative chart.) Browser/server combines many of the advantages of both centralized and distributed computing architectures and is set to become the dominant computing architecture of e-business.

Terminal/host puts a dumb device, the terminal or VDU, on the desktop that depends on a connection to a specific host computer, such as a mainframe or minicomputer. Terminals are directly connected to the host in a "star" configuration, like spokes to a hub. The host manages the data, business logic, and user interface of any application software used, which is presented to the user via the terminal as a series of green-screen text-based forms. A user completes the data entry or data request form and submits it to the host for processing. Data entry that fails during host processing, say due to an input error, is returned to the user for correction. Data requests that succeed return results to the terminal screen or a line printer.

Centralized hosts originally managed all corporate computing at the desktop and can scale to handle hundreds, thousands, or

Exhibit 1.1 Computing Architecture Comparison Chart

Item	*Terminal/Host*	*Client/Server*	*Browser/Server*
Client	Terminal	PC or laptop	Any browser-capable device
Server	Mainframe, mini, UNIX server	PC, UNIX server	Any Internet-addressable device
Network	Direct connection	LAN/WAN connection	Internet connection
Middle-Tier Business Logic	No	Possible	Yes
Database Location	On host	On client (fat) or server (thin)	On server
Application Execution	Runs on host	Runs on client and/or server	Wherever
Application Administration	Host-centric	On client and server	User-centric

even tens of thousands of concurrent users. Today host systems are still vital to the running of most major corporations worldwide. The applications running on them are usually referred to as legacy systems. Terminals have largely been replaced by PCs running terminal emulation software. Hosts also may act as servers servicing desktop users connected to distributed client/server architecture networks to provide access to legacy applications.

The client/server architecture takes advantage of the local processing power of a desktop PC to distribute data processing across client and server computers connected over a network—either a local or a wide-area network (LAN/WAN). Via client/server, applications can take advantage of PC resources to run more powerful graphical application software locally and connect user work groups to dedicated servers optimized to service their business roles. But potentially clients could connect to and use any one of a number of LAN or WAN database or application servers to get data and do their jobs; they do not depend on a specific host or cluster of hosts.

The main benefit of client/server is that it forces software developers to redesign their software so that it consists of separate layers managing the user interface, business logic, and data management needs of the application. Thus software applications become more granular in their design and more flexible in the way they can be implemented across the client and server "tiers" of this technology architecture. However, client/server software often does not perform optimally without a sophisticated technology infrastructure to support it and did not scale well past a few hundred users when used to support demanding applications, such as ERP (enterprise resource planning). Client/server architecture also proved difficult to administer from an IT perspective, requiring administration on both the client and the server(s).

From an e-business perspective, both terminal/host and client/server architectures have significant disadvantages. A diminishing range of packaged software supports the terminal/host architecture and that which is available typically does not support the types of applications demanded by e-businesses. This fact would force businesses to build rather than buy much of their software, a very expensive solution in terms of both cost and time. And while plenty of packaged software runs on client/server architectures, the architecture itself demands top-of-the-line desktop PCs to run well in addition to sophisticated IT resources to keep it performing optimally. Both these architectures encourage the accumulation of expensive fixed assets and participation in non–value-added activities, cost and effort burdens that many e-businesses can do without.

Today's browser/server architecture combines the best of both architectures that preceded it. Browser/server assumes that the client environment is a Web browser and that the server, whether an application server managing business logic or a database server managing data access, can be reached at an address over the Internet. Some advantages of the browser/server architecture follow.

- It can use any client device that can run relatively unsophisticated and inexpensive Web browser software.
- It offers an easy-to-learn and low-resource-intensive graphical user interface experience via the Web browser.
- It can use any kind of server as long as the server device is accessible over the Internet.
- It needs no additional network (LAN/WAN), other than the Internet, to function.
- It does not care whether applications are being run on servers located in house (whether host or "client servers") or run remotely by third parties.
- It is easier to administer as all business logic and data is located on a server and clients can be automatically updated over the Internet if any local software is needed at the client to run an application.

The principal drawback to browser/server computing is that it depends on the Internet, which means it assumes a fast Internet connection is available, that parts of the Internet are not subject to shutdown, that enough Internet bandwidth is available to service the application users with acceptable response times, and that data processing can be managed securely despite running on a publicly accessible network.

Also, even though browser/server applications operate within a Web browser, due to a lack of user interface (UI) standards, many browser/server applications will use different UIs from each other. Unlike the relatively limited UI of green-screen terminal/server applications and the relatively standardized Microsoft Windows UI used by most client/server applications, browser/server only has the basic UI paradigms of Web browsers (back, forward, stop, refresh, favorites, etc.) to build on.

These drawbacks aside, it is not hard to see why browser/server is a compelling computing architecture for e-businesses that want to minimize technology acquisition and administration costs. Browser/server becomes even more popular as more and more packaged software can run in a browser/server mode and most new application software released today assumes that it will function in a browser/server environment.

BEST PRACTICE ACTION ► ARCHITECTURE AUDITS. Most businesses are using a mix of technology architectures, so it pays to conduct a regular technology audit to determine the balance of this mix and its implications from a cost and IT resourcing perspective. Use your next architecture audit to determine if it makes sense to switch any of your terminal/server or client/server architecture applications to new browser/server applications.

CLICKSTREAM FARMING

In today's graphical user interface (GUI) environment, the mouse is now the principal means of application navigation. Application navigation includes accessing and leaving the application, moving around its functions and screens, or picking options and making selections during data-entry or data-query processes.

Internet surfing involves using the mouse to click URL links to travel from site to site and page to page. This rich set of navigation activity is represented by mouse-clicks that in sequence are known as a clickstream. Browser/server applications, such as a Web storefront, generate masses of clickstream data as a result of servicing what can be large numbers of application sessions generated by worldwide user communities.

Fortunately, this clickstream data is collected in log files that are maintained automatically by the Web server software or other specialized applications running on the server. As more and more browser/server applications are used that depend on Web servers for connecting users to business logic and data, clickstream analysis is bound to assume ever-greater importance as a means for analyzing the behavior of anyone, whether internal employees or external business partners, who accesses the applications.

The implications of clickstream analysis for e-businesses are profound. This level of data capture was unusual or simply not available using non–browser/server applications. Now the onus on e-businesses is to harness or farm clickstream data effectively and take advantage of these Web server log files that represent nothing less than a constantly updated data warehouse (a.k.a. Webhouse) ready for analysis.

BEST PRACTICE ACTION ► **ANALYZE YOUR CLICKSTREAMS.** If you have a Web site, you have a clickstream. Do you know what you want to discover from that clickstream? Can you or your ISP already analyze this clickstream? Who is responsible for analyzing clickstreams in your organization, and how do they communicate the results of this analysis to senior management?

EVERYTHING'S A URL

The Internet is a wonderful resource in that it provides a low-cost, global, and publicly accessible network available to every individual and business that can afford a connection. But a key advantage of the Internet for e-businesses is that potentially it makes every business resource individually addressable and accessible. This fact has wide-ranging implications for e-businesses.

Internet addressing takes a number of forms

- An e-mail address (e.g., cfoinfo@btinternet.com)
- A Web site URL (e.g., www.cfoinfo. com)
- A Web page URL (e.g., www.cfoinfo.com/index.htm)
- A device IP address (e.g., 10.10.10.1)

Already, many individuals have their own address on the Internet in the form of their e-mail address. An e-mail address means that an individual can be reached directly via the Internet.

The business implications of this fact are just starting to be understood. Significant concerns exist about an individual's right to electronic privacy. The importance of e-mail addresses is underlined by the fact that already software agents are programmed to search the Web to "harvest" these addresses from Web pages and every Web site visited does its best to collect users' e-mail addresses during their visit. Access to an e-mail address makes one-to-one marketing over the Internet a real and highly cost-effective proposition when you consider that even a telephone number can seldom be linked to an individual with any certainty.

Most businesses now have their own domain name, a Web URL (in fact, a unique IP address) that identifies their organization and makes it accessible to all or selected Internet users. This means that any organization can be reached electronically via the Internet. Like individual e-mail addresses, this address availability raises significant security and privacy concerns. From an e-business perspective, this Web identity means that a business can be reached by its employees and business partners on an anytime, anywhere basis via any Internet connection. The Web URL acts as a gateway into the organization from a business process perspective and is a fundamental enabler of B2B and B2C e-commerce.

Any document or report, database query or result, sound or video recording can now be accessed via its own unique URL, making pieces of content individually addressable over the Internet. This fact is already changing the print and publishing industry and threatening to restructure the music and movie industries. A new generation of "infomediaries" has emerged that over time will disintermediate the business models of traditional content distribution channels such as newsstands, music stores, and theaters. These infomediaries are focused on reintermediating content consumers through Web sites that aggregate and package content in new ways to suit the needs of specific horizontal and vertical markets.

Over time, any number of hardware devices may have their own IP address on the Internet. Today IP addresses primarily identify computer nodes—such as clients or servers—on the Internet accessing or hosting sites on the Web. But other devices, such as printers and scanners or mobile phones and cameras, also can have their own IP address. Printing to and scanning from an IP addressable printer or scanner effectively makes separate fax machines obsolete. E-mail can be sent to an individual mobile phone and converted into voice mail (or vice versa), and a security camera can provide a live feed over the Internet to a monitoring station. Once other devices come online, such as car engines, vending machines, and personal entertainment systems, e-businesses will be able to provide innovative new servicing, replenishment, and content download to users.

We are fast reaching the stage where every business will be able to create a truly universal address book that provides electronic access from anywhere at any time to individuals, partners, content, applications, and devices via a single, centralized URL listing resource.

BEST PRACTICE ACTION ► CREATE AN INTERNET ADDRESS POLICY. Do you have a business policy that defines and determines Internet addressing? Is a company-wide Internet address book accessible on your intranet that includes the addresses of people, partners, documents, and devices so that your employees can take advantage of Internet addressibility?

EVENT-AWARE ENTERPRISES

One view of business is that it represents nothing other than a series of events in a specific order. But strangely enough, few software applications are in fact event-aware. This is likely to become a problem with e-businesses that run with lean headcounts because the skilled people needed to monitor business events manually are in short supply. In this scenario, it makes sense for e-businesses to limit the amount of human oversight that is needed to identify and respond to business events occurring in their business management systems.

The event-aware enterprise depends on applications that let users:

- Define events that are important to their business in the application context
- Apply their own particular sets of business rules to these events

- Direct how the application should respond to these events (the outcome)

It is particularly important for event-aware applications to recognize and action exception events automatically because, by definition, exceptions are likely to be more important than routine events. For example, a salesperson closing an order could be considered a routine event; the same salesperson losing an order might be classed as an exception event. The "closed-order" event may trigger little more than e-mails to congratulate the salesperson and thank the customer for the order. But the "lost-order" event may trigger a complex set of order post-mortem actions to help ensure that the problem does not happen again.

Event-aware applications are also more likely to scale better in response to increasing use because they do not demand the same levels of human intervention as non–event-aware applications. Event-aware applications are already in common use in businesses where regulatory oversight is high, such as financial services. But these applications are not just useful for controlling risks; they are also vital for spotting opportunities that might otherwise be lost in a sea of data. Bottom line: E-businesses that intend to remain lean or highly focused in terms of human resources *need* event-aware applications.

BEST PRACTICE ACTION ► **DEFINE YOUR BUSINESS EVENT CALENDAR.** Even if you are not using event-aware applications now, prepare for the shift by documenting the business events, actions, and outcomes for specific departments, functions, or business processes. The business event calendars you create will help you begin to understand the frequency of certain business events in your organization and make sure that you can implement an event-aware application more quickly.

FOUR FACES OF THE INTERNET

Most e-businesses display four faces on the Internet, reflecting their public and private faces, as shown in Exhibit 1.2.

Exhibit 1.2 The Four Faces of the Internet

Public	Web Store	Web Site	
	Extranet	Intranet	Private

The public face of an e-business includes the corporate Web site, which usually is marketing oriented, and a Web storefront, if it engages in B2C commerce. The Web site usually focuses on "brochureware" and inquiry handling and the Web store on displaying and selling products and services via an online catalog. These public faces may have little or no involvement with the portfolio of business management systems used internally to run the business. However, few of today's businesses would contemplate using a Web storefront with no or limited integration with back-office inventory, order processing, and accounting systems.

The private face of an e-business includes the corporate intranet and extranet. Both intranets and extranets are collections of applications and content made available to users across the Internet via firewall-protected Web servers. A firewall may be a specialist hardware device or a software-only layer that performs the role of gatekeeper between internal applications and content and the Internet. All traffic to and from the Internet passes through the firewall so that this traffic can be monitored. This monitoring can be used, for example, to prevent certain users or data passing through the firewall.

An intranet is targeted at internal employees and provides access to business management applications and services, corporate e-mail servers, and collaborative tools, such as calendars and to-do lists, and corporate knowledge bases housing documents, reports, diagrams, sound, and video. An extranet is in effect a special version of an intranet that provides selective access to the same or a different mix of applications and content to trusted business partners, such as major account customers, franchisees, or preferred suppliers.

E-businesses have to be multifaceted in order to take best advantage of the sales, marketing, and collaboration opportunities that the Internet offers. Every e-business needs to master management of these new Web assets.

BEST PRACTICE ACTION ► THE FOUR-FACES MATRIX. To understand what content and applications should be represented in your four faces and how they overlap, create a matrix with Web site, Web store, intranet, and extranet across the top and content and/or application function access down the side. Doing this helps provide a simple overview of all four of the Internet faces of your business—preferably on a single sheet of paper.

INTEGRATION RULES

E-businesses are likely to function with a complex mix of in-house and outsourced applications combined with Web services delivered over the Internet. Unless these systems and services are closely integrated with each other, businesses are unlikely to get the best value from them.

The traditional batch update of applications, involving periodic file-passing between systems, is easier to manage than seamless application integration but may not cut it in the world of e-business. There will always be a place for batch update in certain circumstances, but, in general, e-businesses and their stakeholders—such as customers and suppliers—are likely to expect and demand near or true real-time interfaces between systems. Analysts refer to this mode of operation as "zero latency." For example, few customers purchasing from a Web storefront would be happy to know they were ordering out-of-stock items or incorrectly priced items. A batch interface between the storefront application and a back-office ERP inventory module could allow this scenario to happen—a situation that almost guarantees customer attrition. A closer, real-time integration between these two systems would most likely prevent this scenario from ever happening and help ensure better customer retention rates.

E-business managers must demand sophisticated enterprise application integration (EAI) technology from their IT people and, wherever possible, leverage emerging integration standards, based on extensible markup language (XML), to facilitate application collaboration and ensure that timely information is always on hand. The issue for e-businesses has moved from integrating internal applications to each other, known as enterprise application integration, to enterprise-to-enterprise application integration.

Today the challenge is to integrate internal applications with external applications and services, located beyond the firewall, and create the new loosely coupled virtual applications that can be reconfigured quickly to adapt to the changing marketplace.

> **BEST PRACTICE ACTION** ► **TOUCHPOINT MAPPING.** Create an application map that displays the touchpoints, or potential integration points, that exist within every mission-critical business system. This mapping helps to identify functions or information that could be used either by other internal systems or by those of business partners who participate in your demand or supply chains.

ISP TO ASP TO BSP

In the early days of the Internet, the goal for most businesses was just getting onto the information superhighway. Internet service providers (ISPs) developed to deliver the on-ramps to the Internet that connected individual users to the Web, hosting Web sites on their own Internet-connected servers and managing e-mail servers for their clients to send and receive e-mail messages.

In the late 1990s, the ISP business model was expanded to include hosting and running specific software applications and renting access to those applications to users who connected over the Internet. These more sophisticated ISPs are known as application service providers (ASPs) because they deliver a specific software product over the Internet. ASPs run, maintain, and support existing packaged applications on their servers, typically offering a portfolio of such applications to users.

Now a new generation of business service providers (BSPs), who deliver a service over the Internet, are complementing ASPs. The BSP is not based on hosting an existing shrink-wrapped version of a software application. Instead, the service may be based on delivering a software application that has been developed exclusively for use on the Web and cannot be bought off the shelf. Alternatively, a BSP may just deliver information, not software functions, that can be used as is or to complement software functions delivered by in-house or outsourced applications. Company credit checking, request-for-bid buying, and online news feeds are all examples of services currently available from BSPs.

The challenge for e-businesses is to leverage all these outsourced business resources to their advantage. Doing so places a major emphasis on the content and performance of the service-level agreements (SLAs) contracted with the service providers. E-business managers must be prepared to manage their business using a mix of in-house applications, ASP applications, and BSP services—something that demands more flexible technology platforms to achieve and a more business-focused IT department to support.

BEST PRACTICE ACTION ► **INVESTIGATE BSPS.** While your business undoubtedly uses an ISP and also may utilize one or more ASPs, how much use is it making of BSPs? Start an initiative to identify BSPs that could help your business function better by plugging gaps or adding value to application functionality or delivering more regular, accurate, or timely information via your corporate intranet.

MATCHMAKING

The Internet is brilliant at matchmaking, either business-to-consumer (B2C) or business-to-business (B2B). Superior matchmaking via the Internet gives buyers a choice and can force suppliers to meet the market on every transaction. In the past, the one-to-one business-to-business model dominated e-commerce; electronic data interchange (EDI) was used to create a connection between two specific business partners only. New Internet matchmaking options, such as e-auctions, enable consumers and businesses to broadcast commerce requests and offers to a worldwide audience.

Examples of Internet matchmaking include:

- **One-to-Many Matchmaking.** Matching one request for bid from a prospective buyer to many potential suppliers via online reverse auctions
- **Many-to-One Matchmaking.** Matching many bidders to one offer via conventional online auctions

- **Many-to-Many Matchmaking.** Matching anyone with goods to barter with anyone else who has goods to barter

The Internet has turned the physical local market square into a virtual global market sphere, so e-businesses have to examine their specific matchmaking needs and determine how Internet matchmaking services can help to improve their current business processes.

Matchmaking Need	*Matchmaking Service*
Expertise to project	Online "e-lancer" service offers
Resource to vacancy	Online resumé bank
Distressed inventory to buyer	Online auction
Advertising to audience	Online banner placement agency

To find individuals matching the expertise profile need for a project, businesses can tap sites that register individual freelancers (or "e-lancers") available for hire. To match candidates to your hiring needs, businesses can search the many job banks on the Internet that contain regularly updated resumé libraries. To clear out distressed inventory (end-of-line, damaged, or surplus items), businesses can invite offers via online auction sites. To make sure their marketing message reaches the right audience, businesses can utilize an Internet advertising infomediary that creates an online campaign to display their business banners across a range of sites with the right visitor profiles.

BEST PRACTICE ACTION ► **MAKE ME A MATCH.** Understand what matchmakers you could use to support key business processes such as buying, hiring, marketing, and selling. Research the Web to find which matchmakers can help you and cost of using their matchmaking service.

PORTALS ON THE WORLD

The Internet could have been designed for the "me" generation, delivering anytime, anywhere access to a vast array of content and services on an individual basis. Individuals and businesses can subscribe to customized news feeds and niche-topic e-mail newsletters, and get alerted to new or changed content on specified Web sites. They can access in-house and outsourced applications or services from BSPs via the Internet. But taking advantage of all these resources demands that users can find and organize them.

Every e-business needs access to Internet search engines to find information and services and portal technology to organize access to that information and those services. Unfortunately, Internet search engines are currently in their infancy and support only rudimentary page-based searching using keywords or simple English sentences. So far there is little search engine technology available to query Web data sources that deliver the dynamic content used by many business Web sites or that uses goal-based searching to find results. But in a world where everybody and everything may be a URL, the need for e-businesses to embrace state-of-the-art searching technology becomes more pressing.

Portal technology is now more widely available, both as a product and as a service, and finding its way into more and more applications as an alternative user interface to corporate applications and content. Usually a portal acts as a role-based front end to a range of internal applications and content and as a means to integrate content and services available externally on the Internet with those available internally. Portals can be customized at various levels—individual, workgroup, or corporate—and to support various roles, such as customer, employee, or supplier. E-businesses are likely to control the access to information and applications not through user interfaces and security of individual applications but through a set of portals that define the world of individual users and workgroups from an information and application access perspective.

BEST PRACTICE ACTION ► **KNOW YOUR ROLES.** Creating effective portals that provide a single gateway to internal and external applications and content depends on a role-based selection process. E-business managers should know what organizational roles they are in charge of and the profile of those roles from an information and application access perspective.

DOCUMENT-LEVEL APIS

We are fast reaching the time when documents will be able to talk. A document stored in an electronic format and structured using extensible markup language (XML) becomes a true information container that can be interrogated in various intelligent ways. XML is a data description, or metadata language. By using "tags" to delimit and surround data items in a document plus separate document "schemas" to explain what those tags mean, XML lets users describe the content and context of data in a document. In effect, what XML delivers is a document-centric application programming interface that enables all kinds of programs to read and interpret that document. So a voice-generation program could literally read an XML document out aloud.

E-Businesses should expect to make every document they generate capable of speaking and, indeed, listening to what other documents say, if not literally at least programmatically. Doing so means adopting XML document description standards sooner rather than later and working toward making all content generated by the business accessible in XML formats.

BEST PRACTICE ACTION ► GET WITH THE (XML) PROGRAM. Research the XML standards initiatives that could impact your industry sector—there is probably at least one—and start thinking about the implications of using such a standard in your day-to-day business. Figure out which of your applications can create XML output and how you can take advantage of it. Do not buy new applications that are not XML-savvy.

The e-business landscape changes fast. If people in your organization are not charged with monitoring the changes, you need to hire analysts or research groups who focus on this task.

CHAPTER TWO

E-Business Management: Going Beyond ERP

Enterprise resource planning (ERP) suites are a fundamental part of the business management technology foundation for any e-business. An ERP suite is generally considered to be a functionally broad and deep suite of integrated applications that service the financial, distribution, manufacturing, and human resource management needs of the organization. This chapter reviews the status of ERP technology from an e-business perspective and examines why e-businesses need to go beyond traditional ERP for effective business management.

Enterprise resource planning was one of the technology success stories of the 1990s—for the suppliers of ERP applications, at least. Brought to prominence by industry analysts The Gartner Group, the idea of ERP was to extend the concepts of manufacturing resource planning (MRP) to the whole enterprise. Thus the premise of ERP is to bring together all the resources of the enterprise to work together holistically.

Suppliers of business management applications, in particular SAP AG, which marketed a mainframe-based business management application called R/2, embraced ERP as a concept to help market functionally broad and deep suites of applications that encouraged businesses to make all or nothing buying decisions. Top-tier ERP application suppliers, such as Baan, J.D. Edwards, Oracle, PeopleSoft, and SAP, grew their businesses dramatically during the 1990s on the back of a boom in demand for ERP suites from many of the world's largest businesses.

Today ERP suppliers are no longer the high-flyers of the world's stock exchanges. Their market caps languish while many dot-com upstarts, with neither the ERP vendors' revenues nor profits, command far higher market valuations. There are many reasons for this, but one is simply the fact that ERP has had its day. Despite solving many of the problems it set out to solve, ERP created a few problems of its own. In addition it was overtaken by the adoption of the Internet for business use. Consequently, industry analysts, users, and even suppliers of ERP see a need to go beyond traditional ERP to respond to the challenge of managing in an e-business environment.

The following acronyms are used in this chapter.

TERM	DESCRIPTION
API	Application programming interface
ASP	Application service provider
BI	Business intelligence
BAPI	Business application programming interface
CRM	Customer relationship management
EAM	Enterprise asset management
ERP	Enterprise resource planning
IT	Information technology
MRP	Manufacturing resource planning
OLAP	Online analytical processing
ROI	Return on investment
SFA	Sales force automation
SME	Small to medium sized enterprise
XML	Extensible markup language

THE RATIONALE FOR ERP

Suppliers originally targeted ERP at large corporations—typically organizations characterized by all kinds of complexity, such as

- Multiple lines of business

- Multinational business operations
- Heterogeneous technology platforms

These organizations have a wide range of business management applications in place. The applications can be home-grown or bought from multiple suppliers of packaged applications; frequently they are customized. They can include a variety of best-of-breed solutions, chosen because they focus on providing exceptionally broad or deep functionality to service a specific business need. Best-of-breed applications are often also termed "point" or "stovepipe" solutions because they service a specific business need and typically are not well integrated with other enterprise systems. The applications can run on technology platforms that include both centralized and distributed architectures.

The primary problem that this mess of technology platforms and applications presents to business managers, and in particular to IT managers, is one of integration. In this scenario, applications often function as information islands; that is, they make it hard to move data from one system to another and even harder to get a composite view of the business that depends on information collected from multiple source systems.

Stovepipe applications managing discrete functions, such as the general ledger of the business, were often out of step with feeder systems. And even whole processing domains, such as finance, distribution, and manufacturing, could be out of step with each other. Frequently, error-prone rekeying of data between systems was required. As a result, information quality suffered, making it harder to manage the business effectively.

By delivering relatively broad and deep sets of application modules within integrated suites, ERP suppliers did help to solve this basic application integration problem. Multiple individual "point" applications were replaced by a single suite from a single vendor running on a single technology platform—typically a client/server architecture utilizing a UNIX-based server platform combined with a Microsoft Windows client on the desktop. All the modules within an ERP suite are more or less tightly integrated with each other. In many cases real-time up-date (as opposed to periodic batch update) between modules is possible.

ERP systems certainly provided a better integrated solution than most previous system solutions in use. But, they did not always replicate the rich functionality set found in the applications they replaced, applications that benefited from many years of enhancement and customization.

THE DRAWBACKS OF ERP

However, ERP suffers from some serious drawbacks that, over time, have begun to frustrate some businesses that have invested heavily in ERP technology. Functional breadth and depth is hard to deliver without software complexity. Many ERP implementations have suffered from long time lines, steep learning curves, and the need to use costly implementation resources to get the best from the system. These difficult implementations have meant that gaining the anticipated return on investment (ROI) from an ERP system can be delayed and that transferring knowledge from implementation resource to internal staff has not always been accomplished smoothly. Product complexity also means that maintaining and upgrading the ERP suite—coping with ongoing product fixes and applying major new product releases—can suck up considerable time and effort from both IT and line-of-business people alike.

In addition, to avoid the hassle and expense of customizing the new ERP suite to the specific needs of the business, many organizations opt to implement ERP as is and bend their business processes to fit the package, rather than the other way around. In some cases, doing this can be very beneficial since the processes supported by ERP systems are often more efficient than the processes in use in the pre-ERP systems and organizations. But in some cases this as-is implementation has meant that process support is less comprehensive, because ERP systems do not include or support every business process in use, or found in the highly customized proprietary applications they are replacing.

And, in fact, until the end of the 1990s many ERP systems themselves acted as information islands in that they provided limited or no means to easily integrate their data and business logic with other complementary applications. In some organizations this led to problems integrating ERP with other legacy and best-of-breed applications that had to continue to run alongside the ERP system. Often users felt that they were being locked-in by their ERP vendor.

Most ERP suppliers have now enhanced their products to provide some sort of application programming interface to their systems. Nevertheless, creating interface programs is never easy and keeping them maintained in the face of regular product updates is a challenging task.

ERP REALITY CHECK

For some organizations, ERP was one of the best things that could have been introduced to make them more efficient overall. For others, the ERP system has not met their ROI expectations. For a few, introducing ERP was nothing less than a costly and possibly disastrous failure.

Despite all the claims, ERP has basically been an expensive fix. ERP was an evolution, not a revolution, a tactical rather than a strategic initiative. Admittedly, ERP solved a number of critical problems with traditional business management systems. ERP helped move IT shops off proprietary hardware platforms and databases onto more open systems and accessible relational databases. It replaced messy combinations of loosely interfaced built-and-bought systems with tightly integrated and relatively complete single-vendor application solutions.

But in the end, from an architecture perspective, ERP is simply another foundation layer that sits above the database, operating system, and hardware. (See Exhibit 2.1.) In reality, ERP software

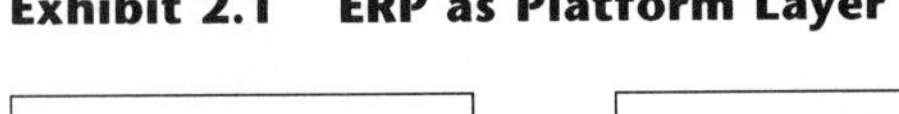
Exhibit 2.1 ERP as Platform Layer

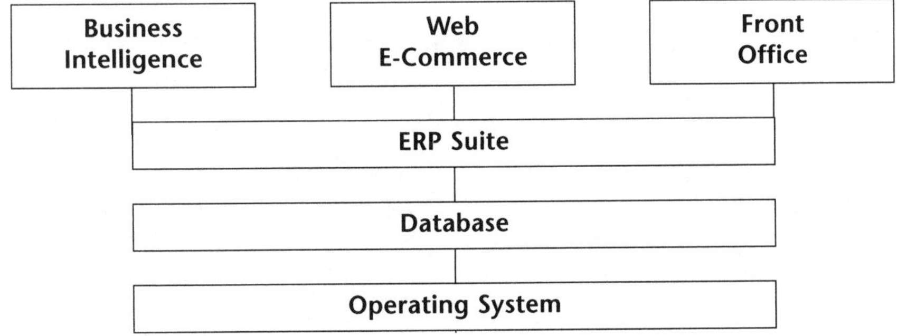

still does not manage all the resources of an enterprise and probably never will. The real return on investment from ERP comes when this foundation layer is leveraged by other maturing application suites, such as those designed to deliver business intelligence, employee self-service, front-office services (sales force automation and customer relationship management), integrated supply chains or Web-based electronic commerce.

> **BEST PRACTICE ACTION** ► **LEVERAGE ERP.** If you have an ERP system in place, treat it like other technology platform components. Look to see how your effort to standardize on a single ERP system can be further leveraged to deliver better business intelligence, integrate with your Web assets, or support front-office self-service initiatives to deliver better customer or employee self-service.

EXTENDED ERP

Toward the end of the 1990s, the functional breadth and depth of even the most complex ERP systems was being tested by demands for the integration of front-office applications to complement the back-office applications traditionally delivered by ERP suppliers.

Front-office applications include sales force automation (SFA) and customer relationship management (CRM) applications that complement existing ERP modules, such as order entry or accounts receivable. (See Exhibit 2.2.) Extending ERP systems to include front-office applications broadens the reach of ERP systems to include sales and service staff. The scope of front-office

Exhibit 2.2 Extended ERP for Managing Customer Assets

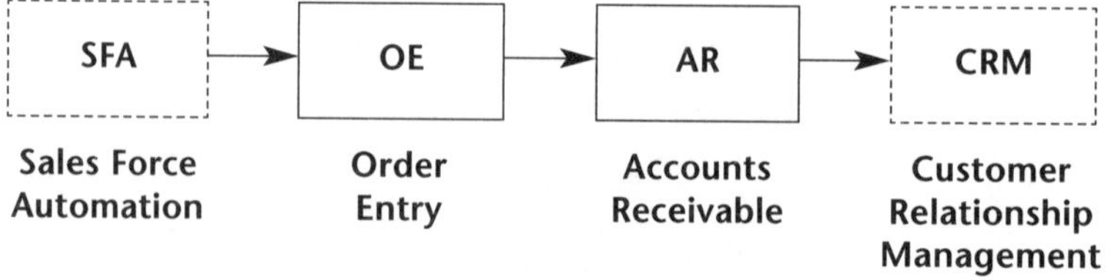

applications also includes the analytical tools used by managers and business analysts to provide information about how the business is performing; often these tools are known as business intelligence software.

Vendors responded by building or buying front-office applications and integrating them into their already complex ERP suites. They also provided data warehouse and other performance measurement initiatives that generally depended on alliances with online analytical processing (OLAP) and business intelligence application vendors to make data easier to get and information easier to assimilate.

As interest in front-office, e-commerce, and business intelligence applications increased as a means to leverage more value from ERP investments, it has become clear that ERP is just another technology that has been turned into a commodity by forces outside its control. Today's ERP systems are being surrounded by a number of applications that transform ERP into a support application for providing better organizational data and information visibility to employees, managers, customers, and suppliers alike. (See Exhibit 2.3.) These add-on applications are adding the value to and creating the real ROI from ERP technology by enabling the ERP system to be used by a wider range of people and businesses.

Exhibit 2.3 ERP Surround Sound

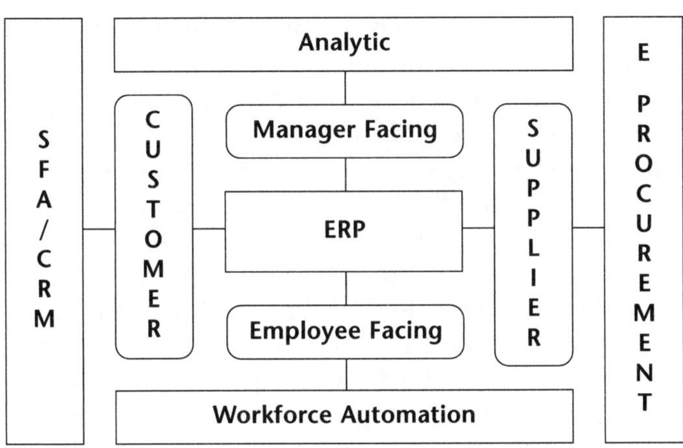

- Applications devoted to CRM and SFA provide a face to customers.
- E-procurement applications provide a face to suppliers.
- Analytic applications provide a face to managers.
- Workforce automation applications provide a face to employees.

BEST PRACTICE ACTION ► **EVALUATE BEST OF BREED.** Always evaluate best-of-breed solutions as an alternative to extending your ERP solution by buying from the same vendor. Many best-of-breed packages now ship with interfaces to the leading ERP systems; therefore, you are taking less of a risk going with a best-of-breed alternative than was the case just a few years ago.

EXTENDED ERP VERSUS EAM

In the pre-ERP days, business management software was organized into functional "silos," such as accounts payable, purchasing, and fixed assets. Vendors of ERP have been instrumental in helping organizations break free of this silo mentality by introducing a more work flow–centric design based on support for cross-module business processes such as procurement and fulfillment. One possible future direction for ERP is to adopt an asset management perspective to the design of business management software. The ERP software could then simply morph into enterprise asset management (EAM) software. In this way the extended ERP scenario shown in Exhibit 2.2 is transformed into something like the customer asset management solution outlined in Exhibit 2.4.

Enterprise asset management requires the reorganization of the functionality of an ERP system around better management of a business asset, such as the customer. Individual functions are assembled around goal-based activities, such as acquiring, accounting for, retaining, and leveraging customer assets. These activities cross the boundaries of traditional back-office ERP modules to

Exhibit 2.4 From Extended ERP to Customer Asset Management

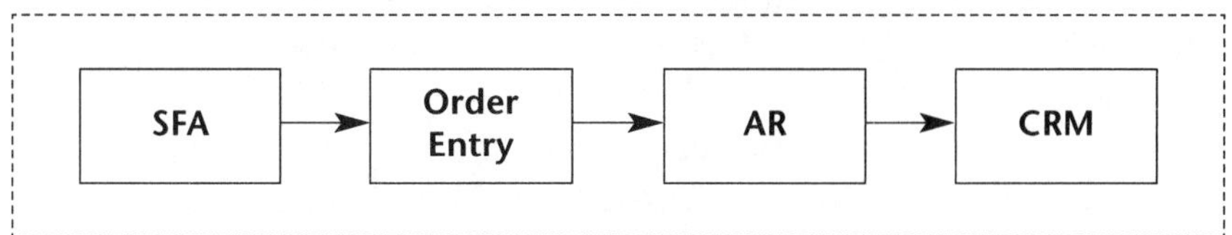

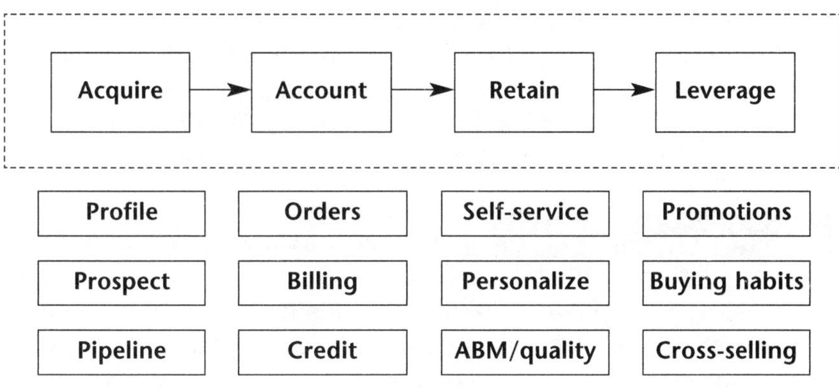

include front-office, analytic, and e-commerce modules for delivering e-procurement and Web storefronts.

> **BEST PRACTICE ACTION ► ASSET MANAGEMENT APPROACH.** Do not expect an ERP system to support an asset management approach without considerable customization of out-of-the-box business processes. Supporting an asset management focus likely will require a considerably different approach to creating a technology solution than an ERP system offers.

FUTURE OF ERP

ERP systems have become a fundamental part of the technology architecture needed to underpin any e-business. It is now practicable for any size of business to take advantage of a fully integrated set of financial, distribution, manufacturing, and human resource applications. But from an e-business perspective the future of ERP looks certain to be service rather than product focused.

It looks likely that many more businesses will choose not to buy an ERP system and go through the hassle of implementation and ongoing system maintenance when they can offload much of this burden by renting applications from an application service provider. Many ERP systems, targeted either at large or small to medium-size enterprises (SMEs), are already available for rent. As ERP leaders, such as Oracle, PeopleSoft, and SAP, make their applications "100% Internet," the distinction between ERP as shrink-wrap product and ERP as Web service will disappear.

BEST PRACTICE ACTION ► **ASP EVALUATION.** If you are considering renting an ERP system from an ASP, take particular care to understand the different implementation models involved, what resources are available to support your users after they sign up such as telephone help and online training, how easy it is to get data in and out of the system, and how much customization, if any, is possible of the system's business logic and screens.

As ERP systems open up their business logic and data to the outside through exposed APIs, the rationale for using best-of-breed systems rather than extended ERP will become stronger, since they will be easier to integrate with the core ERP system. In this case organizations with ERP in place have more reason not to extend their systems by buying from their ERP vendor and instead to buy and integrate third-party best-of-breed applications. Some may even begin to swap individual modules of their existing ERP system with more functional best-of-breed packages.

APPLICATION FRAMEWORKS

Initiatives such as Oracle Exchange, PeopleSoft Marketplace, and SAP's mySAP.com also indicate a future direction for ERP in the e-business world—as the plumbing connecting a network of Web-based application and service providers. While today these initiatives are in their infancy, they could become the ERP systems of tomorrow.

In fact, the whole concept of ERP may become redundant if the current momentum toward application frameworks gathers pace. Application frameworks are designed to allow organizations to create loosely coupled assemblies of applications and services that can respond better to changing market conditions and business needs.

In the hardware arena, Apple Computer pioneered the concept of plug and play to make it easy to connect peripheral devices to a desktop PC. Application frameworks promise to do the same thing for application software by allowing applications and services with clearly exposed and standardized APIs to be snapped together and connected by a set of framework services to create a "virtual application" that combines traditional ERP, best-of-breed applications, and new Web services into a single solution.

These application frameworks in turn depend on the disassembly of ERP applications into pieces that can be reassembled around particular business needs. These pieces may not be pure "objects" in the programming sense (structures that encapsulate both data and the methods to access and manipulate that data). Instead, these pieces may run the gamut from whole business processes, applications, application modules, and functions with which or into which others can be combined.

In the 1990s most ERP applications were monolithic in design—they were not built for disassembly/reassembly. That structure necessitated an all-or-nothing buying, deployment, and upgrading decision by ERP software customers. But today's e-businesses cannot afford to use such inflexible solutions. As a result, ERP suppliers are replacing monolithic designs with more flexible modular or granular deliverables. Some have even surrounded their business logic with Microsoft COM or CORBA-based object "wrappers" to make them appear more like self-standing, collaborative, business objects.

E-business managers must look for more granular design-and-deploy solutions from ERP suppliers that further break down modular software into "cellular" deliverables (see Exhibit 2.5)—

Exhibit 2.5 From Monolithic to Cellular Software

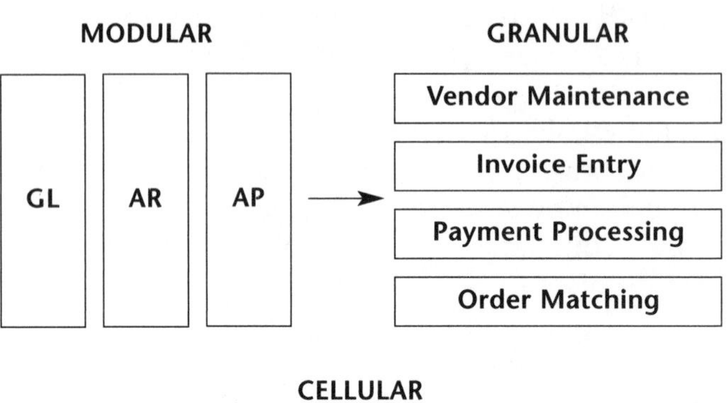

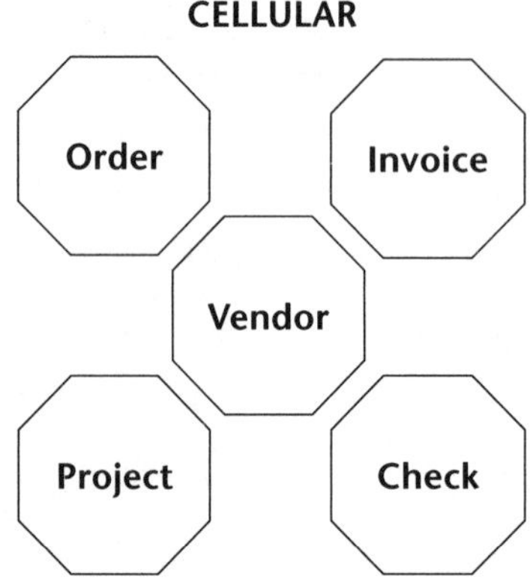

whether the deliverables are called business objects, components, or functional granules. Cellular applications may be built using object-oriented design that mandates the encapsulation of data and business logic by software objects that expose methods used to manipulate their behavior. And since every object must have one or more methods to collaborate with other objects, by definition every cellular application will offer a cell-level applications programming interface that allows far more flexible delivery and deployment options. In future, this cell-level API may well be based on some form of extensible markup language (XML) schema.

A cell-level API also opens up the possibility of building software applications that are assembled to fit the business need rather than the other way around. For example, vendors could offer preassembled cellular frameworks to suit specific industry types, or customers could purchase cell-assemblies in the form of processes or clusters to suit specific business needs. SAP's BAPI (business application programming interfaces) initiative is an indication of the potential of future cellular software to integrate more easily with both internal (i.e., other parts of the ERP system) and external application cells.

For an e-business, ERP is just another set of services that are required to support the real focus of the business, which might be profitable e-tailing (online selling), efficient supply chain participation, or delivering superior customer service. E-businesses today have the luxury of opting to buy or rent ERP services, which enables them to avoid much of the IT-intensive aspects of implementation and allows them to grow into the ERP system and avoid costly system changes every three to five years. Eventually e-businesses can expect to benefit from a new generation of application frameworks that enable them to break the lock-in stranglehold that traditional monolithic ERP systems can have on the business.

BEST PRACTICE ACTION ► **WEB-ENABLED ERP.** When reviewing a prospective ERP solution, e-business managers should focus their attention on these questions: Is the system available via ASPs? Can modules/functions be purchased and deployed on a mix-and-match basis? Has the suite been rearchitected for delivery over the Internet? Does the system come with a rich set of APIs? What support does the system offer for XML reporting and business document exchange?

CHAPTER THREE

Monitor to Manage: Enterprise Positioning System

Every e-business needs its own version of a global positioning system (GPS) in the form of an enterprise positioning system (EPS). A global positioning system is a handheld device that tells you exactly where you are anywhere in the world by cross-referencing your location with orbiting satellites. While any individual can buy a GPS for a few hundred dollars or less, the same kind of device does not exist for businesses. You cannot buy an EPS in a store, and building one is a significant IT and business challenge that all e-businesses must face to stay competitive.

Every e-business must have an EPS because in today's fast-paced business world, every business must strive to operate as a "real-time" enterprise. A real-time enterprise uses monitoring and analytic software to keep track of important events and exceptions that occur in business management systems, ideally as they happen. Real-time monitoring and analytics let managers maintain better day-to-day control of the business and more easily synchronize business operating tactics with business strategy. This chapter discusses the software and the techniques needed to track and monitor the many data collection systems operated by a typical e-business.

BEST PRACTICE ACTION ► **TIMING YOUR BUSINESS.** How real-time is your business? Identify which of your business systems introduce gaps between when the data is recorded and when information is available for decision-making. Determine if it's possible to eliminate these gaps and whether the effort will deliver enough added value to justify the cost of converting from a batch-based to a real-time process.

The following acronyms and terms are used in this chapter.

TERM	DESCRIPTION
Alert	An electronic notification to inform a person that an event has occurred
Analytic software	Software used to analyze data and convert it into information
Clickstream	The series of mouse-clicks used to navigate Web pages or Web sites
Data mart	A subset of a data warehouse focused on a specific business domain
Data warehouse	A database of aggregated information used by analytic software
EIS	Executive information system
EPS	Enterprise positioning system
Event	A condition that managers determine is noteworthy to the business
Exception	An event considered to be exceptional for the business activity
KPI	Key performance indicator
Outcome	The result of applying rules to an event occurrence
Rule	Business logic applied to an event to determine its outcome
Scorecard	Visual representation of key business metrics and their current status
Subscriber	An individual who needs to be informed that an event has occurred

BUSINESS MONITORING

The foundation of any EPS is the use of a combination of monitoring and analytic software. This combination lets managers control an e-business with what industry analysts GartnerGroup call "zero latency"—a minimal gap between the event occurrence and the ability of systems or humans to respond to the event. Ideally, the EPS should operate both within and across the plethora of data collection systems in today's enterprise. (See Exhibits 3.1 and 3.2.) A GPS succeeds because it cross-references an individual's position with more than one satellite. Similarly an EPS can be effective only when it bridges multiple data collection systems to present a more holistic view of the business activities.

BEST PRACTICE ACTION ➤ ESTABLISH YOUR BASE DATA. Do you know what range of data collection systems exists in your organization, and who is responsible for them (the data owners)? Figure this out as the first step in building your own EPS.

There are at least three types of business monitoring: (1) event, (2) contextual, and (3) analytical monitoring. (See Exhibits 3.2 and 3.3.) Each requires a different approach and usually a different set of software tools to implement. Often each of these types of monitoring is used to generate alerts—electronic notifications (usually via e-mail) that alert managers to changes in information status or to exception events that demand some kind of action to take place. An alert can trigger:

- Generation of an e-mail message sent automatically to specified individuals to notify them of a specific condition identified by the monitoring system. The message may include the means to take some action; for example, it may embed a Web URL to allow the recipient to view a report or document resulting from the event.
- Refreshing of a visual information display to reflect a change in information status, such as redrawing a chart to reflect new upper and lower values or causing a value in a spreadsheet to display in red to highlight an exception condition.

Exhibit 3.1 Some Data Collection Systems

System	*Data Collected*
Desktop applications	Document and spreadsheet files
E-mail	Messages
ERP	Business transactions (invoices, payments, etc.)
Web site	Clickstreams
Web storefront	Customer interactions

- An item to appear in a work-flow management system's to-do list or to be displayed on the home page of an employee portal seen when the employee accesses the corporate intranet

Event Monitoring

Event monitoring focuses on trapping some kind of event occurring in your business systems and communicating the occurrence

Exhibit 3.2 Events, Rules, and Outcomes

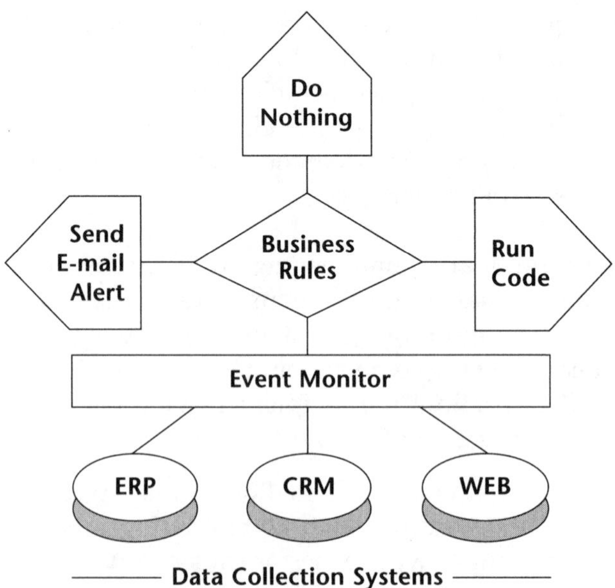

Exhibit 3.3 Analytical and Contextual Monitoring

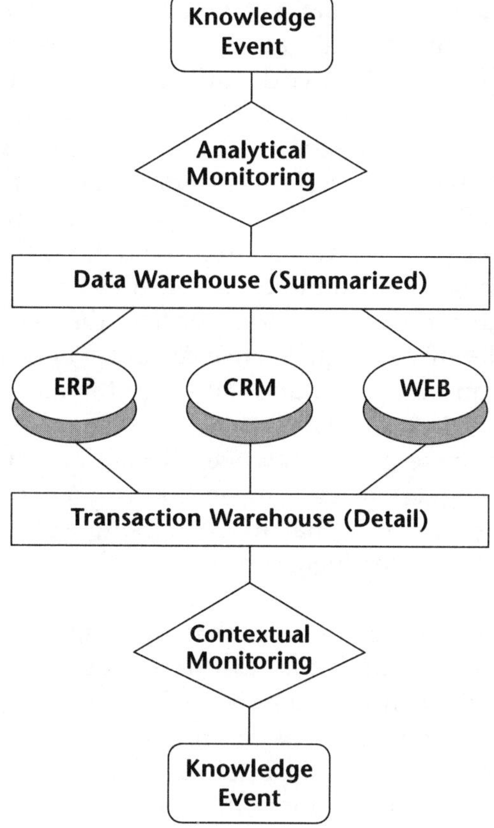

of that event, in the form of an alert or program request, to a person or system that can "action" the event. Event monitoring enables managers to take action quickly rather than find out about an event later, when there is little they can do about the situation. At least five types of events require monitoring:

1. System events
2. Database events
3. Business events
4. Process events
5. Knowledge events

System events are conditions that impact the availability or operation of a system or the individual hardware devices that make up a system. The IT department is generally responsible for managing system events, which can include devices going offline, bottlenecks occurring in network traffic, or software application crashes. Monitoring system events is an important aspect of technology infrastructure management and in particular network and hardware asset management. It is less important in the context of this discussion of event monitoring as a foundation for an EPS.

Database events are conditions that the database management system can monitor. For example, as a result of an insert, the system may update and delete rows/records in the database tables/files. Rules, called triggers, that cause certain actions to take place automatically can be created and stored in the database. For example, triggers may occur when specific types of insert, update, or delete actions take place. However, limitations in the capability of database triggers usually mean that trigger code is used to respond to database events that apply to a single table in the database, limiting their effectiveness for managing complete multi-table events.

Business events are conditions that have significance from a business perspective, such as a "lost order" event or an "exceeds budget" event. Recognizing that a business event has occurred often depends on knowing that certain database events have occurred across multiple database tables or even across multiple databases. For this reason alone, the code associated with business events is usually more complex than the code associated with database events. But both database and business events need access to a set of codified business rules to determine the outcome of the event.

Simple business events are often linked with hitting business-sensitive numeric thresholds, such as when an inventory item hits its reorder level or the entry of a new purchase order exceeds a project budget. The events usually trigger an action or a series of actions that represent a more or less complex work flow of process steps as the outcome or action for the event.

If a business event takes place within a specific business process or work flow, it is sometimes termed a process event, because it impacts the efficiency of a specific process. A process could occur within a work flow contained in a single application, in a work flow that crosses applications, or even in a work flow that crosses organizations—such as collaborative supply chain work flow. Process events often occur as exceptions within the context of a specific business process, causing some form of deviation from the regular process flow to be required to prevent the process from being held up.

Knowledge events are conditions that depend on the occurrence of multiple database or business events being analyzed within a specific context. (See "Contextual Monitoring" below.) The knowledge aspect comes from the fact that the context of the events is used to uncover something that might be hidden when the same events are monitored individually on a one-by-one basis. Detecting knowledge events often relies on more sophisticated software than that used to monitor business events, that includes capabilities such as pattern recognition. Examples of knowledge events include:

- A series of otherwise unexceptional financial transactions undertaken by a customer of a bank could as a sequence be indicative of fraudulent activity.
- Specific patterns of customer behavior recorded at an online storefront over a period of time could highlight a new market opportunity or emergence of a competitive threat.
- Comparing one performance measurement with another—for example, if Web site page views are up but time spent per page is down—could indicate that the page "stickiness" factor is low. If so, the page designer should look more closely at the quality of the content, design, or navigation on the page.

All of the popular relational databases used by applications such as enterprise resource planning (ERP) suites offer database event monitoring through the use of trigger code. Many of these business management applications also offer built-in, rule-based alerting functions to trap business events. "Wizards" walk users through the process of defining all aspects of the event monitoring case. However, both process and knowledge event monitoring systems are thin on the ground and generally costly to acquire and implement.

BEST PRACTICE ACTION ► BECOME EVENT-AWARE. Determine the level of event awareness in your organization. Who or what knows the range of database, business, process, and knowledge events that impact your business? Implement an initiative to understand your organizational events so that you can manage events proactively rather than reactively.

The ability of business management systems such as ERP suites to offer business event monitoring depends on software functionality that can:

- Trap an event as it occurs
- Apply rules to the event occurrence
- Determine and action an event outcome

Trapping the event assumes that event conditions can be defined so that the monitoring software can recognize that the event has occurred. Users must be able to define sets of business rules associated with business events. These rules determine attributes of the event, such as whether it is exceptional or not. An example might be: "Does paying this check cause the account balance to exceed the customer's overdraft limit?" Rules also specify alternate outcomes; for example, "If the value of the purchase is less than $100, then bypass the approval stage, otherwise require approval by the employee's supervisor." Knowledge events demand the ability to create the contextual boundaries for the event monitoring and more complex stepped rule logic to apply to the events as they occur.

The event outcome may be any of the following three examples or a combination of example two and three:

1. Do nothing.
2. Generate a message and send it via e-mail to alert a user to the event.
3. Trigger some application code to do something (i.e., initiate or proceed to the next step in a work flow).

Event alerts have to be used with caution. Individuals can easily become overloaded if they are bombarded with a constant stream of system-generated event alerts.

Contextual Monitoring

Contextual monitoring is a lot more complex than single event monitoring and depends on the use of more sophisticated technology to be effective. The benefit of contextual monitoring is that it helps managers to spot risk or opportunity-related activity in a morass of data so that they can avoid regulatory compliance failure or respond to changing customer behavior or developing market opportunities.

Contextual monitoring is not concerned with monitoring single events; rather it involves exposing and combining multiple events in order to uncover what is called a knowledge event—because discovery of this event delivers real knowledge about the workings of the business. This type of monitoring requires access to a lot of data that may originate from multiple data collection systems. Pattern recognition, fuzzy logic, neural networking, and other advanced software algorithms are put to work to detect patterns and relationships in the data that have significance to your business.

Whereas event monitoring generally works in real time, generating a notification or triggering application code as soon as the event happens in the application or database being monitored, contextual monitoring generally occurs after the fact. This is because raw data first must be gathered from across the data collection systems and put into a specially organized database. (This database is sometimes called a context warehouse.) The context monitoring software is then applied to this large data set on a periodic basis—say at the end of a business day—to expose knowledge events and generate appropriate notifications based on user-defined or system-generated business rules.

Contextual monitoring is used by businesses that have to find knowledge events in large volumes of data that humans on their own, via the use of random or spot checks, could never find or could find only by accident. These businesses include airline, telecom, and utility businesses that process huge volumes of data generated by many consumer customers. Contextual monitoring is also used by businesses subject to strict regulatory controls, such as financial services firms, in order to uncover various types of fraud or unusual customer behavior patterns that could result in the business breaking statutory obligations.

E-businesses tend to deal with more or growing volumes of electronically generated and received data, so contextual monitoring is likely to perform an important role in their EPS, as a means to keep down headcount in the business by reducing the need for human oversight of the data collection systems monitored.

> **BEST PRACTICE ACTION ► BUSINESS ZONING.** Determine if there are any "context zones" in your business that could benefit from contextual monitoring rather than more simplified event monitoring. Figure out whether the opportunities and risks inherent in these zones can justify the implementation of contextual monitoring software as part of your EPS.

Analytical Monitoring

Like contextual monitoring, analytical monitoring also operates after the fact and depends on data culled from many data collection systems to function effectively. The benefit of analytical monitoring is that tactical operational activity can be monitored regularly to ensure that it is in line with overall corporate strategy.

Unlike contextual monitoring, analytical monitoring demands a data warehouse that does not include detailed transaction data but aggregations of data summarized to suit the type of analytical monitoring to be undertaken. This summarized data is then analyzed to determine, among other things, whether the business is meeting its predefined performance targets. Analytical monitoring may deliver its results in the form of conventional reports, as multidimensional "cubes" for analysis by online analytical processing (OLAP) tools, or as regularly updated visual scorecards used to manage a specific aspect of the business.

These scorecards present predefined key performance indicators (KPIs) to managers in logical combinations to help them monitor the performance of a business entity or process such as a territory, product, department, supply chain, or production line. The best-known example is Kaplan and Norton's Balanced Scorecard, which is used to help align the tactical performance of a business with its strategic aims. A key performance indicator defines a specific business metric that management wishes to track on a regular basis. The scorecard presents the results of this KPI tracking in the form of visual "dashboards" that display logical collections of KPIs. These dashboards make it easier for managers to assimilate and act on the information made visible by specific corporate, departmental process, or personal-level scorecards.

BEST PRACTICE ACTION ► KEEP ON TOP OF KPIS. Define the key performance indicators for your own area of responsibility and outline how they could be represented in your own personal scorecard. If your KPIs are already defined, go back and review them, their basis and scope, to see whether anything needs to be changed to reflect new competitive pressures or market trends.

IMPLEMENTING BUSINESS MONITORING

As with most applications of new technology, implementing business monitoring can demand a culture change. For managers used to monitoring their people or activities via a fixed set of month-end reports, the introduction of event, context, and analytical monitoring can come as a bit of a shock. It is important not to overload these managers with alerts and notifications, to carefully personalize the monitoring results to their management needs, and to

BEST PRACTICE ACTION ► DEFINE YOUR EVENT SUBSCRIPTION BASE. Determine exactly who should be subscribed to which events to make sure that event-related information gets to the right people, in the right format, and is distributed on a need-to-know basis.

refocus support staff to react to and act on the results of monitoring rather than undertaking the monitoring activity itself.

How the results of business monitoring are delivered is also important to ensure that managers can assimilate and then act on the events as quickly as possible. Delivering an e-mail notification of an event to a desktop or laptop PC may not be the only way to alert managers to events that need action. Sending the notification by other digital channels—such as by fax or as a short message to a pager or mobile phone—may be better. If the business already has a corporate intranet accessed via a role-based portal, the notification can be supplied as content to the portal's "What's New" page or via some type of electronic to-do in box.

In terms of technology, you may need to do a little or a lot to implement business monitoring. Event monitoring capabilities probably exist already in your database, best of breed package, ERP system, or all three. You just need to determine what events must be monitored, the business rules for the events, and who or what system should get the notifications and in what format.

BEST PRACTICE ACTION ► **CREATE AN EVENT DEFINITION TASK FORCE.** A task force composed of IT and businesspeople should be able to get a quick grip on your event monitoring needs and produce a first-cut list of key database, business, and knowledge events that should be monitored to ensure your e-business is performing as expected.

Contextual monitoring is a different story. First, you should determine if this type of monitoring makes sense for your business and if its potential results will justify the cost of acquiring and implementing the software. If contextual monitoring is appropriate, then you will have to purchase new technology and arrange for the setup and ongoing maintenance of a transaction data warehouse. Thus IT resources will be involved. A dedicated internal team working with the software vendor is required to gradually introduce and then expand the use of contextual monitoring across a range of business systems.

Analytical monitoring may be trivial or tricky to implement. As many business management applications now include such capabilities, you may need to do nothing other than take advantage of functions that already exist in your application. For more specialized analytical monitoring that is isolated from your ERP system and provides cross-application monitoring, you will need a data warehouse (or one or more data marts, subsets of the data warehouse focused on specific business domains) and a business scorecarding tool.

E-BUSINESS ANALYTICS

Business monitoring is an important foundation for an enterprise positioning system, but this foundation must be complemented by a range of analytic applications focused on the specific data analysis needs of individual data collection systems. E-business analytics is about more than traditional business analytics, because in e-businesses, important data collection systems exist outside of the ERP system that houses the target data leveraged by most traditional business analytic software. The data collection systems used for e-mail, supply chain, and e-commerce management need their own specialized analytical systems focused on clickstream, message, and process analytics.

Traditional Business Analytics

Traditional business analytics embraces a wide range of software applications and tools, all of which are still relevant to e-business analytics, including:

- Database report writer tools used to extract and format data from a wide range of data sources to support analytical activities
- Online analytical processing tools used to present and manipulate information on-screen for ad hoc, investigative analysis
- Budgeting and planning applications used to manage the budget planning that most businesses undertake on an annual basis and generate the comparative reporting and

forecasts required to manage a business proactively during the fiscal year

- Financial reporting and consolidation applications used to generate the wealth of operating, management, and statutory reporting that businesses may need to create on a periodic basis, whether that period is a day, week, month, quarter, or year
- Worksheet report writers that add functions to spreadsheet tools to make them more capable of analyzing and reporting financial data
- Reportals (report portal) applications for managing digital report libraries and viewing or launching reports on a self-service basis over the Internet via a Web browser
- Performance monitoring applications used to display high-level financial performance indicators and statistics in the form of business-specific balanced scorecards or executive information system "dashboards"

This traditional business analytic software already makes good use of two key e-business technologies: the Internet and e-mail. For example, business analytic software can utilize an Internet connection in a number of ways to:

- Publish information to Web-compatible formats such as HTML and XML
- View reports or manipulate information in a Web browser
- Access functions, such as launching or refreshing report content in a Web browser
- Send notifications or reports via Internet e-mail; send report URLs in e-mail messages
- Send output over the Internet to devices with an Internet Protocol (IP) address (e.g., a printer)
- Connect to Web servers programmatically to download specific content for compilation into a report

E-mail systems can be used as a means for distributing or collecting business analytic information in a number of ways.

- Reports can be saved to an appropriate file format and mailed to a recipient or recipient group as an attachment to a message; the recipient can double-click the attachment to view it and/or save it to a local disk for further analysis.
- Reports can be saved in HTML/XML formats to a Web server and accessed via a URL link contained in the body of an e-mail message; the recipient can click the URL to connect to the Web server and view the report in a Web browser.
- Report mining engines (software agents that look for exceptions in report data by comparing it to predefined business rules) can generate alert messages that can be distributed via e-mail.
- E-mail can be used to submit reports or other data as part of a collaborative consolidation or budgeting process.

But traditional analytic software is only part of what an e-business will need to embrace as businesses come to depend more on their Web assets, e-mail system, and supply chain collaboration.

Clickstream Analytics

Web assets, such as marketing-centered Web sites and commerce-centered Web storefronts, will play an important role in e-business success. How these Web assets are utilized will become an increasingly important part of overall business analytics and a key part of any EPS.

Web assets generate clickstreams. A clickstream describes the series of mouse-clicks that represent the way a user navigates individual Web pages and Web sites as a whole. The Web servers that store pages and host sites capture this clickstream automatically in log files. As the number, sophistication, and importance of B2C online storefronts and B2B online marketplaces grows, clickstream analytics is becoming a critical discipline for every e-business to master.

A Web site, whatever it is used for, is a major data collection system in every e-business. The site is subject to a wide range of events captured in the clickstream data, and the clickstream represents an obvious context zone for contextual monitoring because the log file is a form of context warehouse.

Basic usage events recorded in a clickstream include:

- Accessing and leaving the site
- Accessing and leaving a specific page on the site
- Time and length of access to page or site
- "Link or load" failures (errors using a URL link or loading a page)
- Patterns of navigation within a page and across the site
- Clicking on banner ads or URLs to link to other sites

Business events that may be recorded in a clickstream include:

- Return of user to site
- Order abandonment
- Payment authorization denial
- Criteria input into the site search engine
- Tracking affiliate referrals

Knowledge events that may be extrapolated from the clickstream include:

- Which pages to emphasize or deemphasize to the user
- The relative "stickiness" factor of an individual page
- Optimum cross-selling or up-selling strategies
- The impact of internal promotions or competitor promotions
- Improving referral rates to the site or to specific pages

While clickstream analysis is important even for marketing-driven, content-focused Web sites, it is vital for sales-driven, commerce-focused online storefronts. Running an online store without clickstream analytics is like running a conventional store with blindfolded assistants—it is impossible to really understand who your customers are, how they behave, and how to service them better.

BEST PRACTICE ACTION ► **ANALYZE YOUR CLICKSTREAMS.** Decide what you are looking for from the clickstream associated with a specific Web site and monitor it regularly to understand and track trends associated with the usage of the site.

Message Analytics

E-mail is a key e-business technology. As the volume and content of message traffic is increasing and expanding all the time, the corporate e-mail system is already a primary data collection system. Apart from being a major consumer of Internet bandwidth and desktop or server disk space, the message data managed by an e-mail system can represent a

- Knowledge base
- Legal liability
- Collaboration audit trail
- Reflection of part of every employee's daily productivity

Message analytics recognizes that this message traffic can represent important information that would otherwise be lost.

As a knowledge base, message databases can be mined using keyword and pattern matching to extract and then assemble bodies of knowledge about specific issues, events, people, or products. As a legal liability, message databases could include data showing that employees are engaged in illegal activity, such as insider trading, or message contents could be used as evidence in legal actions. Message data can be analyzed to look for specific combinations of keywords that are indicative of potential legal issues. These keywords could include the names of individuals, companies, stocks, funds, or products. Neglecting to mine message data for knowledge and legal liabilities is both wasteful and dangerous on the part of e-business management.

BEST PRACTICE ACTION ► **MINE YOUR MESSAGES.** When was the last time you mined your message archive looking for knowledge or potential legal liabilities? If it has been a while, do a test drill looking for a specific product name or the name of your key competitor in the messages.

Messages often form part of a collaboration audit trail, and sending and receiving messages can represent a significant chunk of employee time. Collaborations are often with business partners, customers pursuing service requests, or suppliers working to service procurement needs. The job of message analytics here is to determine how more efficient message routing or automated message responders could help make these collaborations more efficient or less human intensive. Employees receiving or sending high volumes of messages may need help to reduce or better manage this load. Here message analytics can help ensure that people are getting the right messages (so they can be diverted using rules if they are not) and responding only if they need to respond. More efficient message collaborations can help improve customer service and reduce the message burden on individual employees.

BEST PRACTICE ACTION ► **MESSAGE METRICS.** Create some meaningful message metrics for your business, and figure out how your message traffic looks in terms of those message metrics. For example, one key metric is how long it takes on average to respond to a message received from a customer. Aim to reduce the number of messages required to satisfy a customer service request. Create rankings of the people who send and receive the most messages to see who the message monopolizers really are.

Process Analytics

Process analytics is a specific form of contextual monitoring. In this case, the context is a specific business process or work flow, such as procurement or fulfillment. Process analytics is used to continuously improve these business processes by

- Identifying process bottlenecks
- Highlighting process exception events
- Monitoring process metrics for performance measurement

Without process analytics in place, it is hard to determine if any process is in fact operating at full capacity.

Identifying process bottlenecks depends on identifying and monitoring specific nodes in a process for their activity levels. For example, these nodes may be an individual or a location. In the procurement process, a node may be the original requisitioner, the requisitioner's manager, the purchasing department, or the goods-in location. Here you are concerned about factors such as inflow and outflow volumes and time to process items at the node.

Process exception events may be associated with highlighting specific levels of process bottleneck, such as a high number of requisitions awaiting approval, or with highlighting unusual process behavior, such as an increase in orders over a specific dollar value or a high number of requisitions being rejected. Here you are concerned with events such as rejections, returns, inactive states, and hitting thresholds.

Even if process bottlenecks and exception events are identified, there is no way to effect continuous improvement of business processes without creating and regularly reviewing a scorecard for each process. Like all scorecards, the process scorecard depends

BEST PRACTICE ACTION ► GET PICKY WITH PROCESSES. Pick a process, any process, and define the potential bottleneck nodes, exception events, and KPI metrics for that process. Determine if any software is actually managing all, some, or none of these bottleneck events and metrics.

on the definition of a set of process KPIs and on making a manager responsible for these metrics.

You cannot run a best practice e-business without superior monitoring and analytic software in place. And because e-businesses embrace a wider range of data collection than traditional businesses, this monitoring and analytic software also must encompass new areas, such as knowledge event management, contextual monitoring and clickstream, and message and process analytics.

CHAPTER FOUR

Collaborate to Compete

Electronic collaboration between businesses is not new. It is just that before the introduction of the Internet and a universe of commerce-related Web sites, collaboration was a lot harder and more costly to achieve. Its scope was limited to traditional electronic data interchange (EDI) via standards such as EDIFACT or X.12.

Today the world of electronic collaboration is developing rapidly and introducing new technology, new ways of collaborating, and more sophistication into the collaboration process. Electronic collaboration is a skill organizations will have to master to become best practice e-businesses; if they do not, they will be unable to exploit some of the most important opportunities offered by the Internet.

The following acronyms and terms are used in this chapter.

TERM	DESCRIPTION
B2B	Business-to-business commerce
B2C	Business-to-consumer commerce
Community	A group of suppliers and/or customers using a trading hub
EDI	Electronic data interchange—exchanging business data electronically
EDIFACT	A standard used for defining EDI documents or transactions
IP address	Internet protocol address—a specific node on the Internet
RFB/RTB	Request for bid/response to bid

TERM	DESCRIPTION *(continued)*
Trading hub	A Web site for connecting buyers and sellers for online trading
VAN	Value-added network—used to carry EDI traffic between participants
VPN	Virtual private network—connects two points across the Internet
X.12	A standard used for defining EDI documents or transactions
XML	Extensible markup language—used to describe business documents

TECHNOLOGY OF COLLABORATION

Electronic data interchange essentially defined the technology of collaboration until the end of the 1990s. EDI describes the exchange of structured data electronically between businesses—that is, between source and target applications. (See Exhibit 4.1.) Typically EDI software translates data from line-of-business systems to and from standard formats. Standards such as X.12 and EDIFACT have developed that specify the vocabulary, grammar, and formatting blocks of these data exchange messages so that specific types of business documents or transactions can be processed between business partners.

Conceptually EDI remains as important as ever. Yet despite the fact that millions of EDI transactions are processed per year and the value of these EDI transactions is worth billions of dollars, traditional ways of implementing EDI are unlikely to represent the future of business-to-business (B2B) collaboration. There are two reasons for this: disadvantages with traditional EDI and the arrival of the Internet and extensible markup language (XML).

Exhibit 4.1 Electronic Data Interchange

The disadvantages with traditional (pre-Internet) EDI have hampered its ability to become a pervasive standard for B2B collaboration. Traditional EDI had a reputation for being complex and expensive to implement. Costly EDI software was needed to ensure that EDI participants' systems could communicate with each other, and businesses were forced to subscribe to special networks—called value-added networks (VANs)—to communicate EDI traffic securely between collaborating participants. Also, most packaged business systems had to be adapted to work with EDI software since there was limited or no integration between the various systems out of the box.

Although this cost and complexity was much reduced in the 1990s, the upfront implementation cost of integrating the EDI software with line-of-business applications and the ongoing subscription or per-transaction usage costs of the VAN still made EDI expensive, especially for smaller businesses with low-volume collaborative needs. Also, the use of different EDI VANs by different groups of suppliers and customers meant that a business might have to participate in and subscribe to multiple VANs, adding further complexity and cost to EDI-based collaboration.

The Internet has sounded a death knell for traditional EDI in two ways. First, it has provided a means to communicate data electronically between business partners that does not depend on proprietary VANs to carry the data. Also, the Internet has helped to promote a new open data description language, XML (see Chapter 10), that can build on the existing EDI standards and service a wider range of data interchange needs. However, there remain security and bandwidth concerns over using the Internet for this type of business traffic, and the delivery of XML-based document standards is in its infancy.

Collaboration over the Internet for EDI purposes may eventually depend not on VANs but on virtual private networks (VPNs). VPNs do not require dial-in to a special VAN connection but simply use regular Internet protocol (IP) addresses to provide point-to-point communication over the Internet. Anyone with an Internet connection can use a VPN. As VPN software improves in terms of security, ease of setup, and ongoing management, a VPN may become a highly cost-effective carrier both for traditional EDI traffic and for "new" XML-based EDI traffic.

BEST PRACTICE ACTION ► PILOT VPNS INTERNALLY. If you intend to use a VPN to transmit EDI data with your business partners, pilot the concept first by using a VPN to transfer documents and data between parts of your own company. Doing so will help you to determine security, performance, and management issues before you involve your business partners.

COLLABORATION SERVERS

As traditional EDI morphs into the transfer of XML-based documents and transactions over the Internet, additional technology, in the form of a collaboration server, is needed to allow a business to participate in electronic collaboration.

A collaboration server is software specifically designed to manage collaboration processes, including collaborations between business entities and business applications. Collaboration server software may run on a dedicated server computer or as a service on a server computer shared for other purposes. A collaboration server manages a number of tasks including data communication, work-flow management, and process integrity.

Both server-to-server and application-to-application data communication has to be managed. Server-to-server communication involves creating and maintaining a connection between two servers across the Internet. Application-to-application communications involves passing documents or packets of data between an application working with a source collaboration server application and an application working with a target collaboration server.

Work-flow management makes the collaboration work flow visible to and manageable by human users. For example, it uses electronic out boxes and in boxes to channel outgoing documents and information requests/responses and incoming documents and information requests/responses and to route them to the right application or person to take action.

Process integrity capabilities are required to handle the security, reliability, and scalability of the collaboration process. The server software has to create secure ways to communicate what can be sensitive data; it has to treat individual collaborations as discrete process that must either complete or fail; and it has to be able to respond to the rise and fall in collaboration traffic to manage the peaks and troughs of business activity patterns.

A typical collaboration process managed by a collaboration server could take place between a

- Customer (a consumer or business partner) and supplier
- Customer or supplier and a Web trading hub
- Subsidiary of a corporation and another subsidiary of the same corporation

A customer and a supplier can pass documents between them—such as orders, invoices, and payments—as part of a one-to-one supply chain work flow. A customer can send a request for bid (RFB) to a trading hub, or a supplier can send a response to bid (RTB) to a trading hub as part of a one-to-many or many-to-one collaboration. A subsidiary can send a financial statement to another subsidiary for consolidation, send various types of intercompany transactions between them, or conduct other more basic data exchanges required (e.g., to keep subsidiary-level accounting or inventory databases in synchronization).

BEST PRACTICE ACTION ► DOCUMENT YOUR COLLABORATIONS. Do you know whom your collaboration partners are? What range of documents do you exchange with them? Figure out if the full scope of your business collaborations are recognized and which documents could benefit from being exchanged electronically.

Collaboration server software typically includes a transformation engine to translate between data types and formats so any-to-any data mapping and conversion can be supported. For example, Microsoft BizTalk Server 2000 translates between formats such as X.12, EDIFACT, XML and flat-file structured data and also supports vendor-specific document and data interchange formats such as SAP's IDOC documents. Thus one major role of a collaboration server is to act as a universal translator for the data and documents exchanged between collaboration partners.

Collaboration servers depend on other supporting services to work effectively. For example, Microsoft's collaboration server initiative also leverages the company's BizTalk Framework, which consists of:

- BizTalk Framework Schemas that describe sets of XML data tags that can be used by various types of business for exchanging data and documents
- The BizTalk.org Web site, which can be used as a repository for storing, publishing, and viewing BizTalk-compliant schemas, and which contains a community center for users of BizTalk

The aim of the framework is to encourage businesses to create BizTalk-compliant schemas and publish them to the BizTalk.org repository for either public or private (restricted partner) use. Other vendor and user-backed organizations, such as OASIS and RosettaNet, also run similar framework initiatives.

Making use of this type of collaboration framework helps to ensure that:

- XML data exchange is managed in a consistent way.
- It is easier to map data from one business process or document to another.
- Everyone can benefit from access to published, publicly available schemas.

If ERP, CRM, and e-commerce vendors commit to support a specific collaboration server and framework in their products, it will become easier to implement cross-application work flows and data exchange. For example, if ERP application vendors support collaboration servers, it will become easier for businesses using these applications to collaborate with each other electronically out of the box.

A collaboration server can be deployed internally or externally to an organization. When deployed internally, the collaboration server runs within the corporate firewall and is managed by internal information technology (IT) resources. Alternatively, businesses could make use of a collaboration server hosted and managed externally by an application service provider (ASP). Documents and data generated by internal systems are then sent over the Internet to the ASP server, from an in-house application (i.e., an ERP system) that generates some kind of standardized XML output. The ASP service then passes the document on to the target partner over the Internet or transforms the document first before passing it on to another business using the hosted collaboration server's transformation engine.

In order to use collaboration servers, applications must import and export data in XML to make providing and receiving data possible. Many software vendors have announced, demonstrated, or delivered XML data import/export from their applications. In most cases these vendors focused initially on core sets of business documents, such as orders, invoices, and payments. Over time, all transactions created by or imported into applications and any query or report output from an application are likely to be available in XML format. This development will dramatically increase the potential scope of EDI between businesses.

BEST PRACTICE ACTION ➤ GET COZY WITH COLLABORATION SERVERS. If you have not done so already, get a collaboration server set up so that your IT people can get familiar with the use and potential of this software, perhaps by setting up pilot collaborative ventures with other parts of your own organization to exchange documents and data.

INTERNET AS INTERMEDIARY

The Internet plays a critical part in the new age of electronic collaboration as an intermediary for both B2B and B2C collaboration and commerce. In this respect the Internet both disintermediates traditional B2B and B2C relationships and reintermediates these supply chains by introducing new types of dot-com intermediaries that depend on the Internet for connecting businesses to their partners or customers.

However, the Internet as intermediary is more than just a low-cost way of transmitting EDI documents between businesses. The Internet makes it possible to create

- Virtual markets
- Niche communities
- One-to-many collaboration chains

These new aggregations of business partners depend on the transformation of traditional supply chains into new value chains that combine and take advantage of both virtual and physical (clicks-and-mortar) assets.

VIRTUAL MARKETS

A virtual market is an aggregation of suppliers and customers around a specific Web site, often termed a trading hub or online marketplace, which focuses on trading a horizontal or vertical set of products and/or services. The market is virtual because it depends for its existence on a Web site and on its customers and suppliers having an Internet connection so they can participate in this market from anywhere at any time. The market maker may be a software vendor, a third party, or a group of participants within the market itself.

Software vendors such as Ariba, CommerceOne, Oracle, and SAP maintain virtual markets primarily for the benefit of customers who use their e-commerce or ERP software. In this case the market is usually tightly integrated with the market makers' software application, such as an e-procurement application that literally acts as an "on-ramp" to the online marketplace and its community of suppliers and customers. In this way the market maker creates a community that is focused specifically on the needs of its application users.

Third-party market makers act as hosts for a market and take their cut from per-transaction or subscription fees from participants in the market. Internet auctions, such as eBay.com or QXL.com, are examples of virtual markets managed by third parties who simply provide a means for suppliers (with an offer) and customers (who wish to bid) to trade with each other.

Alternatively, market participants, either suppliers or customers, may own the market. Many virtual markets servicing vertical industries are owned by groups of suppliers that supply the market—a mode of operation that has the potential to become dangerously close to a cartel. However, a virtual market such as that established by napster.com for distributing music electronically is essentially created and owned by its customers—an operation that demonstrates the possibilities and power of viral marketing. As you might expect, both types of virtual market have already attracted the attention of regulators.

Collaboration with a range of virtual markets is certain to become an integral part of normal business operations within the decade simply because, over time, there may be no good reason to buy or sell certain goods and services except through these virtual markets.

BEST PRACTICE ACTION ► GET REAL WITH VIRTUAL MARKETS. Identify existing virtual markets that either compete with your business or provide an opportunity for your business to collaborate with others to sell your goods or services. Then get involved with the markets and communities that your suppliers and customers use.

NICHE COMMUNITIES

The Internet facilitates the creation of niche communities—aggregations of like-minded people collaborating for pleasure or profit. Any e-business can turn this fact to its advantage by creating, sponsoring, or participating in niche communities to sell its products or services or to promote a brand identity. Creating and maintaining a community creates a sense of identity between individuals and the products or services at the heart of the community.

For example, a niche community may be created around a specific product or a message associated with that product that

- Packages specific information about the product for the target community

- Creates a means for participants to provide feedback regarding the product
- Collates other independent content to reinforce product benefits/messages

It is incumbent on e-businesses to create or sponsor these niche communities themselves; otherwise other people will do it for them and intermediate between the e-businesses and their customers. The Web has dozens of independent e-opinion sites, where consumers rant or rave about products and services they have used. Owners of the products and services discussed have little or no control over the impact of these sites; they could gain more benefit from a niche community site that they create or sponsor via a reputable third party. In the future, corporate Web sites are unlikely to be single XYZ.com destinations but portals to a constellation of niche community Web sites designed to support specific current products, services or branding messages.

BEST PRACTICE ACTION ► **NICHE YOUR WEB SITE.** If you have a corporate Web site, look at how you can splinter it into a series of niche community sites that promote specific products, services, or branding messages. If you are about to create a corporate Web site, consider how to design it as a collection of niche communities rather than a monolithic single entity.

ONE-TO-MANY COLLABORATION CHAINS

The Internet is making it easier for businesses to participate in not just one-to-one collaborations but in one-to-many collaborations as supply chains become more visible and accessible electronically.

Traditional supply chains have suffered from a lack of visibility. If lucky, a customer might have visibility into a distributor's system or a distributor into a manufacturer's system. Even this visibility could depend on participation in a closed-community supply chain dependent on a subscription-based value-added network. This type of supply chain visibility focused on one-to-one collaborations.

The Internet is providing the means for creating more flexible collaboration chains that offer significantly more visibility to all participants. For example, it is possible for a customer to initiate a collaboration chain that bounces a request for a product not just to a distributor and then a manufacturer, but also through links to virtual markets, multiple distributors, and manufacturers as part of the same work flow. The effect of replacing a single distributor or manufacturer connection with connections to one or more virtual markets potentially expands the possibilities of the collaboration chain exponentially.

Participants in a bid-driven collaboration chain—customer, distributor, or manufacturer—all have a better chance of sourcing the product they want at a price that has been fully conditioned by market forces. This is unlikely to be possible using traditional one-to-one supply chains. There is also no reason why this collaboration chain should not work equally well in reverse. A demand-driven collaboration chain lets manufacturers or distributors plan what to make or inventory by allowing them to poll distributors and customers to ascertain demand for particular products and services. In this case a customer request for bid is turned on its head to become a manufacturer or distributor request for demand.

BEST PRACTICE ACTION ➤ **REPLACE ONE-TO-ONE WITH ONE-TO-MANY LINKS.** Examine how your collaboration chains could benefit from connection to one or more virtual markets as collaboration chain participants and how you might be able to exploit virtual markets to create request-for-demand visibility.

Today, when customers send an order to a supplier, they rely on the supplier to figure out if the items on the order can be delivered. But when the supply chain becomes literally a chain of collaboration servers passing XML requests and responses between them, the supply chain process collapses into a single work flow that could take just a few minutes to complete. (See Exhibit 4.2.) In this scenario, it is quite practical for a customer's order at the front end of the supply chain to trigger a manufacturer at the back end of the supply chain to make another batch of goods. In essence, the electronic work flow enabled by a group of

Exhibit 4.2 Bouncing Along the Supply Chain

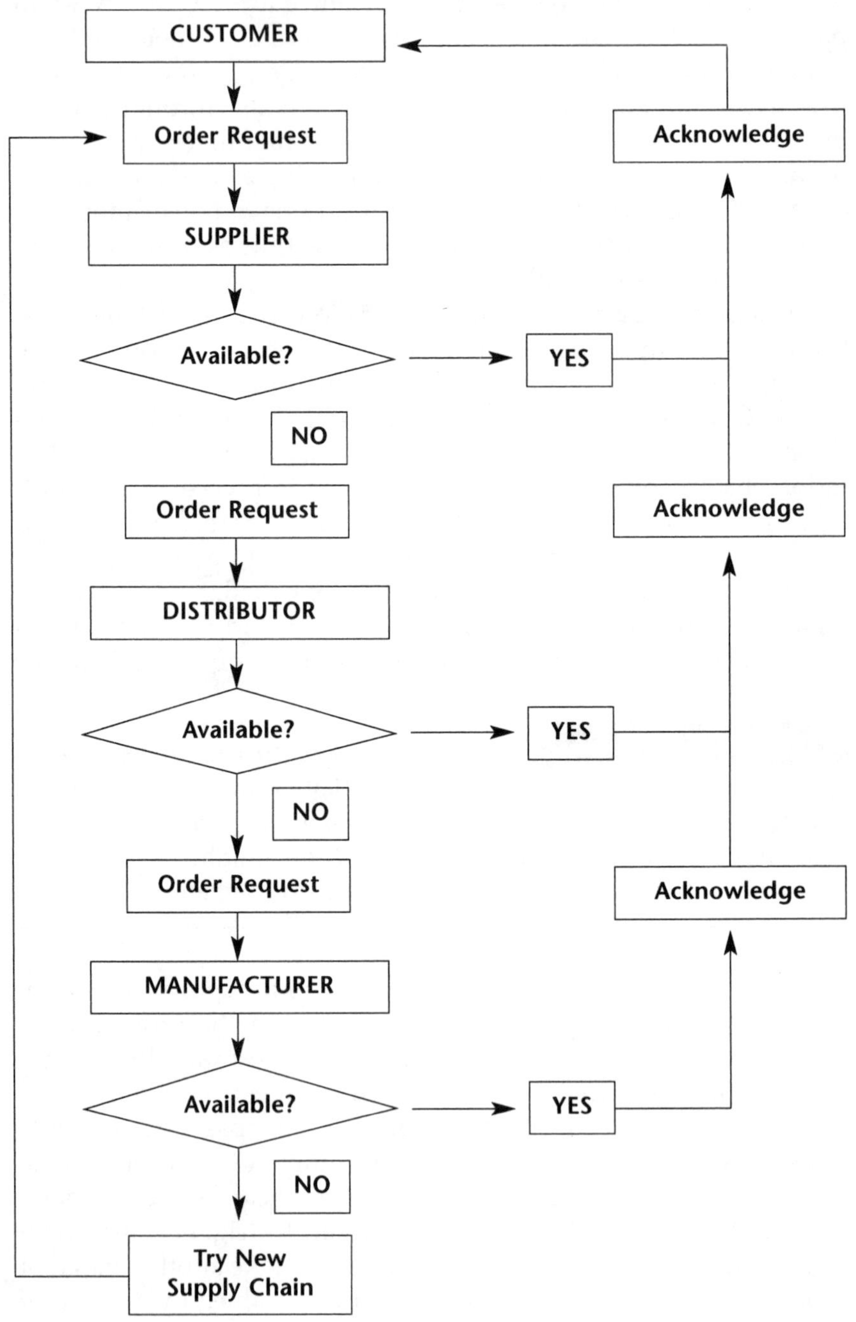

loosely coupled collaboration servers connected over the Internet makes the whole supply chain transparent to the customer, by polling each participant automatically following some predefined business work flow logic built in to the original XML-based order document.

With this transparent supply chain, if a customer's collaboration server figures out that an item cannot be delivered as required via one supply chain (i.e., set of connected business partners), it can then test the same order on another supply chain. This action implies that what matters to the customer is not the supplier per se but the supplier's own supply chain. If this supply chain is limited, say by not making use of XML or Web trading hubs, then suppliers may find themselves discarded in favor of others who can support more sophisticated supply chain execution.

BEST PRACTICE ACTION ➤ SUPPLY CHAIN EXPOSURE. How visible is your supply chain? Can you bounce a customer request to your own supply chain partners or to a trading hub that you participate in? Can trusted customers and suppliers query your inventory systems programmatically to determine if inventory is available or needed?

"VIRTUAL" APPLICATIONS

The use of collaboration servers could also help trigger the end of packaged applications as we know them. In any case, the world of packaged software is in for a shakeup over the next few years for these reasons:

- More applications will be rented from ASPs and run over the Internet.
- More added-value services will be delivered over the Internet by business service providers (BSPs) that only require an Internet connection to be used.
- Businesses will be unable or unwilling to wait for line-of-business application vendors, such as ERP vendors, to respond to changing market conditions with the functions businesses need to maintain their competitive edge.

At the moment, the focus of B2B collaboration servers is to pass transactions or business documents between them for routine e-commerce processes. But in the future these collaboration servers could be used in a much more fundamental way, such as to enable businesses to create and use "virtual" applications.

In this environment, business and IT managers will benefit from a more flexible software solution that lets them assemble virtual applications quickly in response to changing business needs and the rapidly developing world of Internet computing. These virtual applications are made possible using application frameworks designed to let businesses "plug-and-play" in the way that they combine in-house and outsourced applications together with BSP services. A fundamental enabler of this virtual application scenario is the use of XML to link applications and services together. In the future, every application will become best of breed and the concept of a tightly integrated single-vendor ERP system will be an anachronism.

Efficient electronic collaboration is certain to be a vital skill for e-businesses to master. Make sure you are familiar with the technology of collaboration—XML (see Chapter 10) and collaboration server software—and that you review your current supply chains to see how they could be impacted by the variety of collaboration opportunities offered over the Internet.

CHAPTER FIVE

Customer Relationship Management

Every business must focus on the needs of its customers and practice effective customer relationship management (CRM). E-businesses are learning to be more focused on their customers by instilling a customer-centric culture and making more use of broader and deeper CRM technology. But because e-business increasingly involves doing business over the Internet, a high priority is to focus on e-customer relationship management (eCRM). Unlike regular "walk-in" customers, e-customers maintain their relationship with an organization mainly or wholly electronically. This demands both a "clicks and mortar" response to CRM—that is a relationship managed both via the Internet and via physical offices, stores, warehouses or call-centers.

The following acronyms and terms are used in this chapter.

TERM	DESCRIPTION
B2B	Business-to-business commerce
B2C	Business-to-consumer commerce
Business partner	A trusted "corporate" customer supplied via set credit and billing terms
Cart	A virtual shopping cart that represents orders placed on a Web store
Catalog	An item catalog hosted on a Web server for online browsing and buying

TERM	DESCRIPTION *(continued)*
Consumer	An individual customer paying online using a credit/debit card
CRM	Customer relationship management
EBPP	Electronic bill presentment and payment
eCRM	E-customer relationship management
E-customer	A customer who interacts primarily electronically with a supplier
ERP	Enterprise resource planning
Fulfillment	The process of delivering a product or service to a customer
Interaction channel	A means of communicating with a customer electronically
Self-service	Providing the means for customers to serve themselves via the Internet
SFA	Sales force automation
Web store	An online storefront accessible over the Internet

THE WORLD OF CRM

Competition for customers is intensifying. Customers themselves are becoming more picky and choosy about products and services. Their buying habits are changing as more business is done electronically and there are more options to place their business. To deal with this, organizations are being forced into an about-face to realign their operations around the customer and learn to manage customers as long-term assets rather than one-time projects.

The first and most demanding step in this realignment is to instill a customer-centered attitude enterprise-wide that recognizes

- Increased competition means that customer expectations are being raised. They expect better-quality service and products and more and easier ways to buy, return, and service products.
- Higher consumer sophistication means that customers are demanding more personalized products and services. They

expect more customization of product and service deliverables and more input into the design and delivery of products and services.

- Customers are a source of knowledge about needs, trends, and expectations in specific marketplaces. Their feedback should be solicited at every opportunity and evaluated and analyzed regularly.
- Internet-savvy customers are proving more inclined to help and service themselves if they can. Providing self-help and self-service capabilities is likely to help lower operating costs and foster a closer connection between your business and the customer.
- Customers expect (and may be legally entitled to) privacy relating to the use of their information for purposes other than order processing. They also may want the option to be informed about events or offers that are relevant to their buying profile.
- The availability of the Internet in the home and in business means that customers can source their products and services from a worldwide rather than a local or country-specific supplier community. Their range of choices is expanded dramatically.

> **BEST PRACTICE ACTION ➤ GET TO KNOW YOUR CUSTOMERS.** Organize a seminar that refreshes the perceived wisdom about your customers and their needs and expectations, and introduces emerging trends in your key markets. Hold the seminar at least annually and make it attract a cross-organization audience, so it is not just a sales and marketing boondoggle.

Clearly these are just some examples of how the changing nature of customers is changing the way organizations must respond to them. Specific organizational initiatives are needed to realign an organization around the customer. Such initiatives include:

- Remapping organization charts to focus less on functions or operations such as accounting and sales and more on the effective management of business assets such as products and customers

- Retraining everyone in the organization to make sure they understand how they interface with the customer and how they can help ensure that a customer's experience reflects the "face" that the organization wishes to project
- Creating customer advocates whose function is to foster a partner-collaborative rather than supervisor-confrontational relationship with the customer and to act as the interface between customer groups and internal customer-servicing functions such as production, sales, or accounting

BEST PRACTICE ACTION ➤ REALIGN THE ORGANIZATIONAL CHART. Review your organizational structure and identify those individuals whose primary function is to manage the customer asset better. If such individuals do not exist, or if the answer is "our sales and service reps," consider establishing some new or realigned positions charged with customer asset management or customer advocacy.

Once these types of initiative have been completed, then CRM technology is needed to help enable CRM to work in practice. The aim of CRM technology is to provide broad support for CRM activities as well as deep knowledge of the customer and customer groups, markets, and market knowledge. This deep knowledge can only come from integrating CRM activities, to cut the number of databases used to manage CRM, and using a single customer identifier for each customer asset in order to get a true picture of their worth to the organization (a significant challenge for larger organizations with multiple lines of business).

POSITIONING CRM TECHNOLOGY

While the CRM technology marketplace only took off in the 1990s, already it is a confusing mix of products, concepts, and acronyms that reflect a very wide range of tools and applications as shown in Exhibit 5.1.

Not all CRM software is used in-house. Call centers and help desk functions are frequently outsourced to specialist providers who provide both the facilities and people for the call or service center. Also, new application service providers (ASPs) are emerging who deliver CRM-related Web services, especially for sales force automation and e-customer management.

Exhibit 5.1 CRM Tools and Applications

Tool or Application	*Description*
Marketing	**Software for Targeting Customers**
Lead sourcing	Prospect profiling and lead generation
E-marketing	Marketing campaign, event and knowledge management
Solicitation	Mailshot, e-mail newsletter, and alert list management
Sales Force Automation	**Software for Acquiring Customers**
Contact management	Voice, e-mail, fax, and letter interaction
Pipeline management	Progressing sales leads from inquiry to order
Opportunity management	Micromanaging specific sales opportunities
Customer Service	**Software for Retaining and Rewarding Customers**
Call center/help desk	For handling customers calls and support
Field service	For managing service requests (warranty, repair, etc.)
Loyalty management	For managing customer loyalty programs
E-Customer	**Software for Managing E-Customer Relationships**
Storefront	For building and maintaining an online storefront
Portal and personalization	For self-service access to content and functions
Interaction management	For communicating with the e-customer by channel

CRM: TARGET, ACQUIRE, AND RETAIN

A useful way to cut through CRM technology hype is simply to focus on finding ways to use technology to help target, acquire, retain, and reward customers. (See Exhibit 5.2.) Ultimately what most businesses want from CRM technology is assistance in finding more of the right customers, in keeping them satisfied, and in preventing them from defecting to competitors.

CRM: Targeting Customers

Targeting customers is about finding and reaching them. But a prerequisite is to understand what customers you are looking for by creating customer profiles to target ideal matches to your products and service offerings. You can build these profiles only by analysis, both of your existing customers and of the markets servicing potential customers you want to reach. Therefore, you will need to spend some time using analytic tools to assemble the baseline information about current customers to create an ideal customer profile. To attack new market sectors, you will need to get on the Internet to research what constitutes the profile of a "target" customer, customers you want to reach but have not sold to or serviced before.

In practice, finding and reaching means making use of lead sourcing and e-marketing software and services. The Internet now supports a number of lead-sourcing sites that trawl online databases containing mailing lists and company profiles to deliver a list of what salespeople call "suspects" that match your profile request. Once you have a list of suspects, you can use e-marketing software to reach these suspects and convert them into "prospects."

Exhibit 5.2 Target, Acquire, and Retain Customers

Target →	Acquire →	Retain
Profiling	Contact Management	Call Center/Help Desk
Lead Sourcing	Pipeline Management	Field Service
E-Marketing	Opportunity Management	Loyalty Management

E-marketing software helps you to create and manage marketing campaigns—based both on direct mail and on e-mail—that reach out to these suspects (or to existing customers) and gather supplementary information that causes a suspect either to be discarded or converted into a prospect. This e-marketing software also helps you to build a knowledge base about customers, segments, and markets that can be referenced online and used to manage the sales and marketing documents, such as brochures and fact sheets, that are sent to or viewed by customers.

> **BEST PRACTICE ACTION** ➤ **PUBLISH YOUR PROFILES.** Make sure you have profiles of your ideal or target customers. Update them on a regular basis, and make sure they are easily accessible, via your corporate intranet or document management system, to the people who need to understand these profiles.

CRM: Acquiring Customers

Sales force automation (SFA) software focuses on acquiring customers. Although SFA includes a wide range of additional functions, it is centered on three key activities: contact, pipeline, and opportunity management.

Contact management, in an SFA context, manages the inflow of prospects generated by marketing, by customer service and account manager staff, and via self-generated inquiries from prospective or existing customers. The contact manager helps salespeople to track telephone, e-mail, and fax interactions with the prospects and undertake specific contact-related activities such as snail mail or e-mail solicitations and managing individual or group appointment calendars.

Every organization uses different criteria, but at some point a prospect is ready to move into the sales pipeline. The term "sales pipeline" describes the work flow that manages the conversion of prospect into a customer or an inquiry into an order. The pipeline has a number of stages, such as:

- Information sent
- Demonstration

- Reference site visit
- Product trial
- Contract negotiation

The job of pipeline management software is to make this pipeline visible for salespeople and their managers to help them identify bottlenecks, focus in on pipeline imbalances, and assess the true value of the pipeline from a revenue perspective.

Certain prospects in the sales pipeline may be further identified as "opportunities." These opportunities can represent high value, key-win prospects, or major-account customers—in fact, any prospect that demands special attention. Opportunity management software lets salespeople and managers identify these prospects and micromanage them to ensure that the right amount of attention is focused on their needs. This micromanagement may include sending special information packs, arranging additional site visits, or involving executive-level staff in the sales process.

BEST PRACTICE ACTION ► **THE WEB SFA OPTION.** If you want to add pipeline and opportunity management to your current contact management system, do not expect to get these functions from the same vendor or simply look for a broader SFA package. Instead investigate new Web-based SFA solutions that can deliver these functions for a monthly fee. These Web-based solutions do not require in-house software implementation, which is likely to be disruptive to the sales force in the short term.

CRM: Retaining Customers

Once the SFA software has helped to acquire the customer, the focus of CRM switches to retaining that customer. In fact, customer retention begins right at the point customers are acquired by means of a welcome letter, e-mail, visit, or telephone call to make them feel valued. But customer retention depends largely on your ability to service their ongoing needs. This is where help desk, call center, and service center software comes into play. Integration with ERP systems is also critical to make sure that service people have all the information they need to service customers effectively. Reps need to know when customers have/have not paid their bills, are/are not within their credit limit, or did/did not order a certain item, information that usually resides in the ERP system.

BEST PRACTICE ACTION ► **FIRST IMPRESSIONS COUNT.** Make sure every new order automatically triggers a letter or e-mail to customers thanking them for their business, points them to appropriate sales and service resources, and makes them an up-selling or cross-selling offer that can be exercised via your Web store.

Help desk software depends on the ability to respond to customer inquiries quickly through access to an online knowledge base. If an answer is not immediately available, the software can manage the escalation process to route the question to an appropriate resource electronically and also can manage how a response is delivered (e.g., by e-mail or scheduling a voice call or service visit). Call center software is necessary if you have a high volume of customer calls that needed to be monitored, queued, and allocated across a community of service reps. Service center software is used to manage maintenance or warranty contracts to coordinate service requests with a field-service force and to make sure that service level agreements are upheld.

Many businesses do not run customer retention software in-house but outsource it to specialist call center operators or Internet-based help desk providers. Whether you run this retention software in-house or via an outsourcer, you must receive reports to analyze what can be a high volume of customer interactions so management can identify trends and exceptions in the data.

BEST PRACTICE ACTION ► **DON'T IGNORE YOUR DIALSTREAM.** Call or service centers and help desk data represents a significant "dialstream" that can be converted into a knowledge base of customer feedback. If you are not extrapolating knowledge from this dialstream, you are ignoring a vital aspect of customer analytic activity.

Software certainly can help to automate many aspects of the customer relationship and support an organization that wants to sell more and service their customers better. But CRM software will fail to deliver a significant return on investment if it loses the human touch and if the organization is not already realigning around the customer before the technology is implemented.

E-CUSTOMER RELATIONSHIP MANAGEMENT (eCRM)

E-customers interact with a business primarily electronically. There are two types of e-customers:

1. Business partners (e.g., customers with an existing credit relationship) who want to collaborate electronically using self-service ordering or who order via Web trading hubs (which put business customers in touch with B2B suppliers using EDI or XML-based document exchange as the primary interaction medium)
2. Consumers who are browsing and buying from business-to-consumer Web stores, placing orders directly through self-service ordering, and paying for them using credit cards or other payment methods over the Internet

Whatever the electronic connection, B2B or B2C creates a distance between organizations and their customers that did not exist when relationships were maintained by visiting a store or meeting a salesperson. Traditional methods of targeting, acquiring, and retaining customers—even with the help of CRM technology—must be modified to suit the specific demands of e-customers. For example, the CRM software must be able to communicate with customers across a range of electronic interaction channels, including e-mail and pager. And to be fully effective, e-customer relationship management (eCRM) also requires a holistic approach to selling to and servicing the customer that does not depend on separate front and back-office information islands but depends even more on a fully integrated CRM/ERP solution.

BEST PRACTICE ACTION ► **SOLICITING E-CUSTOMERS.** Do you have an eCRM strategy to put into practice that taps into the growing number of consumers and business partners who want to interact electronically with your business? Are you tracking e-customer versus traditional customer activities and evaluating them, or do you have a plan in place to invest in technology that enables and supports eCRM?

Targeting E-Customers

The world of the e-customer is focused on the Internet with its Web stores, niche communities, and collaborative trading hubs. Targeting e-customers must revolve around activities that go beyond traditional lead sourcing and mailshots to

- Maintain one or more Web stores either as individual Web addresses or as participants in an online mall managed by a third party
- Sponsor, support, or participate in online communities where messages and content that advertise your brand, products, or services can be communicated and placed
- Sponsor, support, or participate in online trading hubs where your items can be included within a catalog that can be searched by e-customers looking for a specific product or service
- Place banner advertising on the sites of independent content providers, communities, or trading hubs, and making sure your Web stores can be found by the most popular search engines and have a prominent position in their search result pages
- Create incentives to encourage all your customers, especially e-customers, to provide you with their e-mail addresses and permission to sell to them electronically via e-mail solicitations, alerts, and newsletters
- Establish traffic-passing affiliate relationships with other complementary Web-based storefronts and content and service

providers to benefit from their traffic reaching your affiliate partner Web sites

While traditional CRM targeting activities also can be used with e-customers, targeting e-customers is unlikely to be fully effective without engaging in some or all of the above-listed activities.

> **BEST PRACTICE ACTION** ► **CREATE A STRATEGY FOR TARGETING E-CUSTOMERS.** Use the points listed as the foundation for the tactical delivery of this strategy. Set a target to get the e-mail addresses of every existing and new customer, then create an opt-in campaign to deliver news, alerts, and offers to these customers via e-mail.

Acquiring E-Customers

Acquiring e-customers depends less on traditional sales force automation (SFA)–based software and methods and more on the sophistication of Web stores and participation in trading hubs.

Visitors to Web stores, whether the store supports B2B or B2C customer activity, are more likely to buy (be acquired) and revisit (be retained) if

- The store mixes commerce with both content and community to create a true "destination" site that e-customers will want to return to.
- The store uses personalization technology to customize what e-customers can see and do based on profile and prior behavior patterns so that customers feel they are being treated as a "market of one"
- The store has an easy-to-navigate structure with a powerful search engine that can locate products and services to buy not just by name but by code, keyword, category, and other criteria that customers use
- The store minimizes the amount of data entry required by customers, especially returning customers, by storing contact

data and preferred payment methods to get as close to Amazon.com's patented "one-click" ordering as possible

- The store displays items that are in stock or informs customers online if they are not and displays correct prices that reflect any special terms negotiated with customers or based on customers' profiles
- The store can intelligently apply tax and shipping charges based on the contact data supplied by the e-customers and offers online payment with minimal delay caused by checking customer creditworthiness
- The store alerts e-customers to special offers or clearance sales and uses every item in the catalog as an opportunity to up-sell or cross-sell customers other goods and services while they are online

BEST PRACTICE ACTION ► THERE'S NO SUCH THING AS TOO MUCH FEEDBACK. Get focus groups of online shopping neophytes and experts in front of your Web store for feedback on the issues just outlined. Have your store regularly audited by an outside source to track performance, availability, content freshness, broken links, and other measurable elements of the site. Solicit online feedback when customers leave the site or complete an order to assess their mood at the time.

Retaining E-Customers

Studies have shown that many consumer e-customers leave or do not revisit Web stores or abandon their online shopping carts before buying due to factors such as lack of information or the need for reassurance from a human being. Similarly, business partner e-customers will walk due to a lack of technology capability on the part of the supplier. To combat this, an e-business must manage e-customer interactions in a more sophisticated way by offering customers multiple options. Exhibit 5.3 outlines the range of interactions required to support consumer eCRM and Exhibit 5.4 outlines the same for business partner eCRM.

Exhibit 5.3 Consumer eCRM Interaction Management

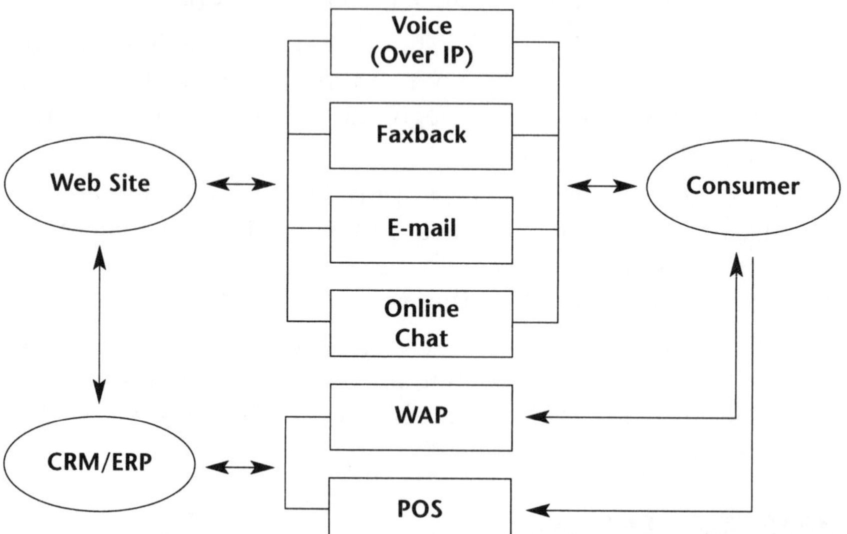

Consumer eCRM interaction management requires that a customer at an online Web store can push a button or click a URL from the site or a specific page to:

- Initiate a voice-over-IP telephone call (or at least trigger an automatic callback) to talk to a sales/service representative while online
- Request a fact sheet or product specification or diagram to be faxed via an automated faxback service directly from the Web page
- Get access to buying guides or independent content, such as product reviews, to provide "rich context" for the buying decision
- E-mail a copy of the page to a friend or colleague who might be interested in the product or service or request an e-mail alert when the price or specification of the product/service changes by simply clicking a button and entering an e-mail address

Exhibit 5.4 Business Partner eCRM Interaction Management

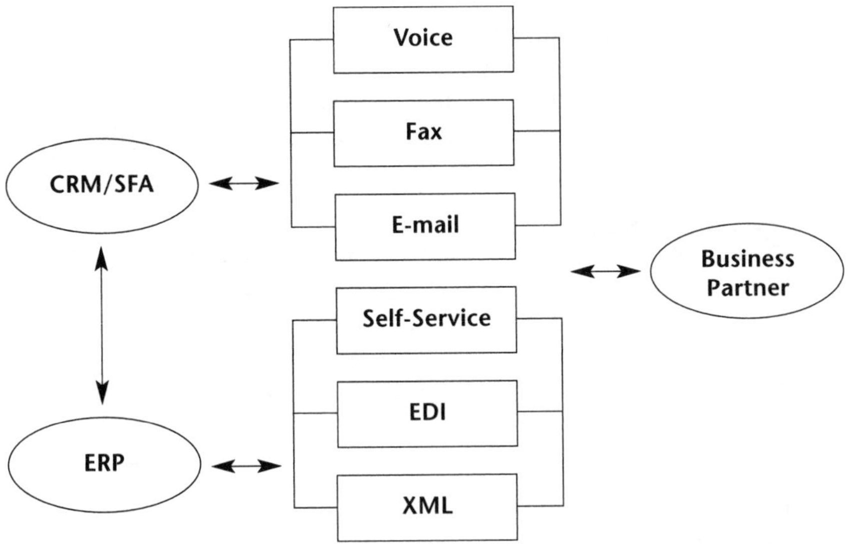

- Open up a chat window to initiate an online chat session with a sales or service representative to conduct a question-and-answer session
- Search a frequently asked questions (FAQ) database that relates specifically to the product/service being considered for purchase
- Access a feedback database built using input from other customers who have purchased the product or used the service
- See a progressively more detailed picture of a product (a visual drilldown), or view the product from different viewpoints (e.g., perspective or color) or even take a virtual reality product "tour" to walk-thru or around the product

Other electronic interactions with customers include those via wireless technology, such as wireless application protocol (WAP) and point-of-sale (POS) devices. WAP lets customers make price or in-stock checks or place and track orders via a mobile phone or other handheld device. POS devices upload remote buying activity from cash registers or vending machines to a central location.

Keeping track of and consolidating all these interactions into a single CRM database is way beyond the scope and capability of traditional SFA-focused contact management software and demands the use of new-generation e-customer interaction management software.

> **BEST PRACTICE ACTION** ► **GET INTIMATE WITH INTERACTIONS.** Figure out which types of interaction make sense for the products/services you are selling, select the types you think are the most useful, and run a trial to determine whether its use actually impacts sales or just causes e-customers to spend longer at your site.

While interactions with business partner customers can still largely be managed within traditional SFA software, one-to-one B2B and many-to-one B2B interaction via a traditional electronic data interchange store and forward message hub or a new Web trading hub requires a whole new level of software. This software needs to be capable of sending and receiving either or both traditional EDI messages and new XML-based documents to facilitate interaction between trading partners or between a trading partner and a hub, for example, to

- Receive and send orders to or from a trading partner or hub
- Upload or download catalog data to or from a trading partner or hub

E-customers who expect this type of e-commerce interaction will avoid relationships with suppliers who cannot support traditional EDI or XML interactions. They will involve other partners in their supply chains.

THE IMPORTANCE OF ERP INTEGRATION

No CRM or eCRM system can be complete unless it offers some level of integration with an ERP, or equivalent, system. As Exhibit 5.5

shows, this ERP connection is important in at least three areas: inventory, order processing, and accounts receivable.

Integration with an inventory system helps to ensure that e-customers have access only to items and item configurations that they are authorized to buy, see only items that are in stock or available to allocate to their order, and buy at prices that have been agreed between the trading parties. Integration with an order processing system helps to ensure that e-customers can create and track their own quotations and orders and buy at the latest prices based on agreed discounts. Integration with an accounts receivable system helps to ensure that e-customers can pay their bills online or order goods and services only if they are within their available credit limit.

Many CRM, eCRM, and Web storefront packages come with some type of ERP connectivity built in. Even with these connectors, however, further integration effort is normally required to close the loop between the two systems. Without ERP integration, databases and business logic will have to be created and maintained in two places to manage certain processes, especially online selling. This arrangement results in

- Duplicate effort, possibly involving the rekeying of data
- A higher likelihood of error and discrepancies between the two systems
- Difficulty in getting a single, complete view of customer activity
- A tendency for a single customer to have multiple identifiers

Exhibit 5.5 ERP Connection

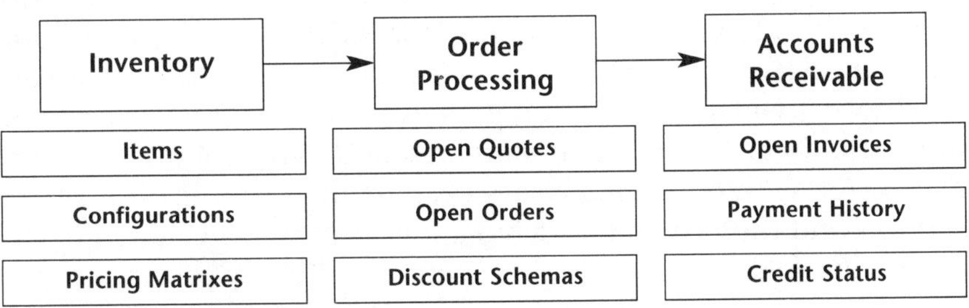

- A need for a data warehouse to consolidate data for analysis purposes

Even with well-integrated CRM and ERP systems, it is still possible that customers could have more than one identifier. It is unlikely that there is one single customer record; at least two are common—one in the ERP system and the other in the CRM system. One or other of these records acts as the "master" in the relationship between the two systems. Also it is unlikely that, except in the form of a data warehouse that stores aggregated data, one single database includes all customer interactions at a detailed level. So even for e-businesses it may not be practical to achieve the CRM nirvana of a single customer identifier system-wide that uses a single customer "master" record and accesses a single database that contains all CRM-, eCRM-, and ERP-generated customer interactions.

BEST PRACTICE ACTION ► **SYNCHRONIZE YOUR STOREFRONT.** Select Web store software that offers as close to real-time integration with your ERP system—especially the inventory, order processing, and accounts receivable modules—as you can get. Storefronts that depend on e-mail to transmit orders and batch updates of item availability and pricing information are only suitable for businesses with low online sales volumes and infrequent inventory product and price changes—or businesses willing to use armies of people to keep the two systems synchronized.

However, maintaining connectivity between an online storefront and an ERP system is more problematic if an ASP hosts the storefront and the ERP system is run in house. In this scenario there is likely to be a batch update process between the storefront and the ERP system. Real-time price and availability price and inventory availability checking is harder to achieve without duplicate databases being maintained and synchronized in both places. As XML-based interfaces become the norm for both Web services and traditional packaged applications, this challenge will be less onerous. Eventually it may essentially disappear, as both systems will in fact be running as hosted services provided by the same ASP.

CLOSED-LOOP eCRM

Ultimately one aim of a best practice e-business must be to include as many customers as possible in a closed-loop eCRM model like that outlined in Exhibit 5.6. Here the aim is to manage all interactions electronically, via call and service centers, Web sites and Web stores, and to store all these interactions in a database.

For commerce interactions specifically, the aim is to automate as much of the fulfillment process as possible by allowing all customers to place and track orders online, to create and track service requests online, and to monitor the shipping and returns process online. Finally, the use of electronic bill presentment and payment (EBPP) software allows customers to pay bills online and have much of the labor-intensive cash receipt process (in the supplier's ERP system) automated via electronic funds transfer (EFT).

Currently, creating this closed-loop eCRM is a difficult task and depends on the use of CRM or eCRM software, and ERP and supply-chain management software with sophisticated self-service capabilities, and the creation of an EBPP portal or interaction with a third-party EBPP "consolidator" to manage the EBPP process. While it is unlikely that this effort is viable for most small to medium-size enterprises (SMEs), it should be in the vision of every SME for the near future.

Exhibit 5.6 Closed Loop eCRM

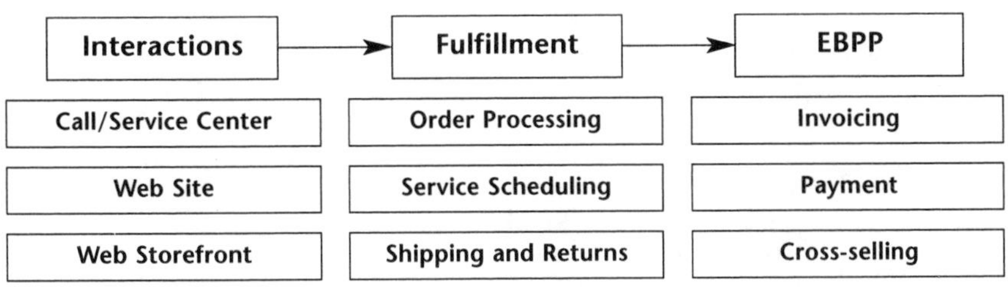

BEST PRACTICE ACTION ► **CLOSING THE LOOP.** Can you close the eCRM loop for certain types of customers or for the delivery of certain types of product or service? While it may not be possible to do this enterprise-wide for every customer and offering, you may be able to gain some experience with closed-loop eCRM by slicing-off a part of your relationship management and investigating how to manage all interaction, fulfillment, and EBPP activities electronically.

CHAPTER SIX

E-Procurement

The procurement process, from requisition to payment, is currently undergoing a period of revolutionary change. The primary change drivers can be summarized as:

- A focus on improving the procurement of nonmanufacturing supplies
- The introduction of new e-procurement software and services
- The sourcing of products and suppliers electronically via Web trading hubs
- The incorporation of Internet auctions into the procurement process
- The emergence of new extensible markup language (XML) standards

Through use of new e-procurement technology and processes, e-businesses have the opportunity to reduce the cost of the procurement process, to source from a wider range of suppliers at lower prices, and to encourage individual employees to conform more closely to corporate procurement policies and practice.

The following acronyms and terms are used in this chapter.

TERM	DESCRIPTION
Catalog	An online catalog of goods and services to browse and buy from
EFT	Electronic funds transfer
E-procurement	A paperless process for buying goods and services from suppliers
Hub	A Web site that acts as the matchmaker between buyers and sellers
Maverick buying	Buying nonrecommended products from non-preferred suppliers
MRO	Maintenance, repairs, and operations
OBI	Open buying on the Internet (document exchange standards)
Order (PO)	An order placed with a supplier to deliver a product or service
ORM	Operational resource management
P-card	Purchasing card used to consolidate low-value, high-volume purchases
Preferred supplier	A supplier with whom special buying terms have been negotiated
Requisition (PR)	A request from an employee to purchase a product or service
RFB	Request for bid (sent to a reverse auction hub)
RFO	Request for offer (sent to a conventional auction hub)
RTB	Response to bid (returned from an auction or hub site)
Three-way match	Matching the order (1) to the receipt (2) to the invoice (3)

E-PROCUREMENT: PROCESS, COSTS, AND ROLES

E-procurement is a way of sourcing suppliers and buying goods and services that depends on new practices, new technology, and new services accessed over the Internet. To understand e- procurement, it helps to be clear on the process, costs, and roles involved in corporate procurement.

E-Procurement Process

E-procurement software supports the procurement process from req to check (requisition to payment). A key aspect of e-procurement software is that as much as possible of the buying relationship with a supplier is managed electronically, rather than on paper. A typical e-procurement work flow involves the steps outlined in Exhibit 6.1.

BEST PRACTICE ACTION ► IDENTIFY YOUR PROCUREMENT GAP. Undertake a gap analysis of your current procurement software to determine how far it is from the best-practice work flow outlined in Exhibit 6.1. Investigate the choices you have to source e-procurement technology from your current ERP supplier, a specialist e-procurement vendor, or by using an e-procurement service offered by an application service provider (ASP) or a business service provider (BSP) over the Internet.

Note that for this process to work effectively, the procurement software (or service) must have:

- Access to online catalogs that can be viewed via a Web browser or interrogated programmatically to select goods and services to buy
- A role-based electronic approval cycle and a rules-based exception handling capability to manage the e-procurement work flow
- E-mail connectivity between the participants in the process and access to Web-based self-service tracking pages to monitor the e-procurement process

Exhibit 6.1 E-Procurement Work Flow

Work-flow Step	*Description*
Requisitioning	Employees requisition the goods or services they need directly via an online catalog that contains only approved suppliers and products for those employees, using centralized business rules mandated by management.
Order Submission	The order is auto-approved using systematized business rules or approved by a manager via an electronic approval work flow and submitted electronically to the vendor either individually or as part of an order consolidated and submitted by a purchasing specialist.
Order Tracking	The order progress can be tracked online using a self-service URL link and/or via order status "alert" e-mails sent automatically to the employees or purchasing agent via the supplier's own fulfillment system.
Receipt Processing	Receipts can be booked using a self-service form via a Web browser on an anytime/anywhere basis and payment on receipt used to settle the vendor bill without the need for a three-way match process that includes waiting for the vendor invoice to arrive.
Payment Processing	Payments are sent electronically to the vendor either on receipt or on completion of an invoice match stage, based on a payment approval work flow monitored by a member of the finance department.
ERP Update	The e-procurement system can transfer accounting data for the purchase either directly or via a batch process to a specific ERP system to make sure it is accounted for correctly.

- The ability to generate and transmit payments electronically to settle invoices in a paper-free way
- Automated interfaces to keep the financial or enterprise resource planning (ERP) system synchronized with the e-procurement system (or service)

Few traditional purchasing modules found in packaged accounting software sold in the late 1980s to mid-1990s supported some or any of these capabilities without the need for add-on software. So for most organizations, implementing an e-procurement initiative should be subject to a clean-sheet approach. See Exhibit 6.2 for procurement process and roles.

E-Procurement Costs

A number of costs are wrapped up in the procurement process, including the cost of

- Staffing internal purchasing departments
- "Maverick buying" by employees
- Paper forms, handling, and storage
- The time taken to perform procurement roles
- Delays in the procurement process
- Managing three-way matching
- Cutting checks to pay vendors
- Maintaining large vendor master files

Exhibit 6.2 Procurement Process and Roles

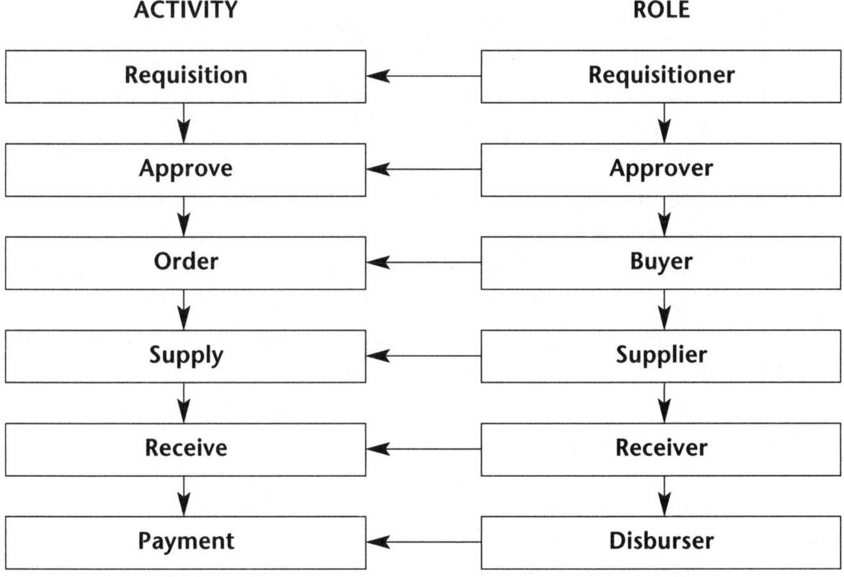

- Poorly informed negotiations with suppliers
- Poorly managed supply contracts

BEST PRACTICE ACTION ► ENUMERATE YOUR PROCUREMENT COSTS. Put a number on these costs in your organization. You may be able to cost-justify an e-procurement initiative on basic cost savings alone.

E-procurement can cut or even eliminate these costs by

- Systematizing corporate buying polices as server-based business rules and applying them consistently to every purchase requisition, order, or payment to reduce the need for oversight and force employees to comply with corporate procedures
- Using online forms, electronic in boxes, to-do lists, and e-mail alerts to reduce the time it takes to create, approve, and monitor purchase requisitions and orders and largely eliminate paper from the process
- Implement pay-on-receipt practices to pay vendors automatically and electronically via electronic funds transfer (EFT) to eliminate the three-way match process
- Provide a more complete purchasing data set and the analytical tools required to understand the procurement process better and to supply the statistics needed for more informed negotiations with suppliers

Clearly the cost savings that can be effected within larger enterprises—those with high employee counts, many procurement transactions, and many suppliers in addition to complex corporate buying procedures and policies—are likely to be more significant compared to those that can be effected in small to medium-size enterprises.

E-Procurement Roles

The procurement process involves a number of roles (see Exhibit 6.2). The aim of e-procurement is to make the performance of these roles as easy and as effective as possible. (See Exhibit 6.3.)

Exhibit 6.3 E-Procurement Role Descriptions

Role	*Description and Aim*
Requisitioner	The employee requesting the product or service who needs to be able to start the procurement work flow as easily as possible and adhere to corporate buying policies
Approver	A manager with the authority to approve the purchase of specific goods and services who needs to be able to manage approvals quickly, easily, and on an exception-only basis
Buyer	A procurement specialist with the knowledge to know whether multiple requisitions should be consolidated into single orders or part of blanket orders from which items are "called-off" when needed, then sent to a single supplier or to a hub
Hub or Supplier	A trading hub or individual supplier that ideally wants to receive orders electronically in a format that is compatible with internal systems and to maintain the procurement relationship electronically from receipt of order
Receiver	The requisitioner or a "goods-in" person at a warehouse who confirms receipt of the product or service and needs to be able to confirm receipt easily and quickly and hand off any exceptions that occur
Disburser	An accounting person who approves and initiates payments to hubs or suppliers and needs to be able to quickly approve and effect payments electronically

E-procurement supports these roles by encapsulating them within the procurement work-flow management and providing electronic in boxes, to-do lists, and e-mail alerts plus the exception-management and escalation-handling tools that help minimize the likelihood of role bottlenecks occurring.

OPERATIONAL RESOURCE PROCUREMENT

The focus of many traditional procurement applications has been on the sourcing and supply of parts and components used in manufacturing processes. The need for tight integration with manufacturing-led work flows meant that purchasing operational resources or services was not well supported or was made overly complex. Procurement software was hard to use, especially for the new generation of service businesses.

> **BEST PRACTICE ACTION ► WHERE IS YOUR PROCUREMENT FOCUSED?** Is your procurement focused on supporting manufacturing, operational resources management (ORM), or acquiring services? What is the relative mix between these areas? E-procurement technology is likely to deliver most benefit to organizations with significant ORM procurement activities.

Operational resources (OR) are the products needed by employees to run an organization day to day, such as office supplies or computing hardware and software. Poor support for OR buying means that many employees try to circumvent corporate purchasing systems and buy goods "on expenses" or indulge in maverick buying, as e-procurement software vendors call it. These activities circumvent corporate buying policies and undermine preferred supplier relationships.

Also, buying services is different from buying parts to store as inventory and call off for use in manufacturing or systems integration projects. But the effects of downsizing and an increasing focus on core competencies has meant that more businesses are making more use of outsourced services to fulfill organizational roles. Consequently, many businesses are forced to manage the procurement of services outside their main purchasing system with all the drawbacks this nonintegrated approach entails.

E-procurement software aims to provide better support for the buying of both operational resources and services, not components or assemblies used in manufacturing. In its focus on operational resource procurement, e-procurement software is different from previous generations of purchasing software in that it is:

- Employee centered
- Catalog based

Employee Centered

Employee centered means that the software is designed to be used by employees rather than just a limited number of purchasing professionals. Improved user interfaces, anytime/anywhere accessibility via a Web browser, and simplified purchasing work flows are all part of making e-procurement software employee-centered. Early-to-market e-procurement vendors, such as Ariba, pioneered the concept of "walkup" user interfaces to ensure that an e-procurement application could be part of every employee's desktop application set.

Employee-centered applications ensure that more employees do more of their buying using procurement systems that help enforce corporate procurement policy and practice through the use of centralized business rules and standardized work flows. This in turn should reduce maverick buying, make better use of contracted supplier relationships, and prevent the purchasing department itself from becoming a procurement process bottleneck. In addition, it makes the whole chore of buying operational supplies or project-related services more enjoyable for individual employees.

Catalog Based

Catalog based means that e-procurement software depends on the use of an online catalog, rather than an ERP inventory database, as the primary means for selecting which suppliers to use and what products or services to buy. A catalog is an online resource that makes buying corporate goods more like the conventional online buying experience of a Web storefront.

The catalog database itself may be stored and browsed locally or stored and browsed remotely via a supplier or trading hub Web site. (See Exhibit 6.4.) If a local catalog is used, the content can be regularly refreshed electronically via a download from a supplier or trading hub Web server. Or a local catalog items may include links to Web pages on a supplier or trading hub Web server in order to provide the latest, new, or in-depth information (i.e., detailed product specification sheets) via a point-and-click action from the items catalog page.

Exhibit 6.4 Local and Remote Catalog Management

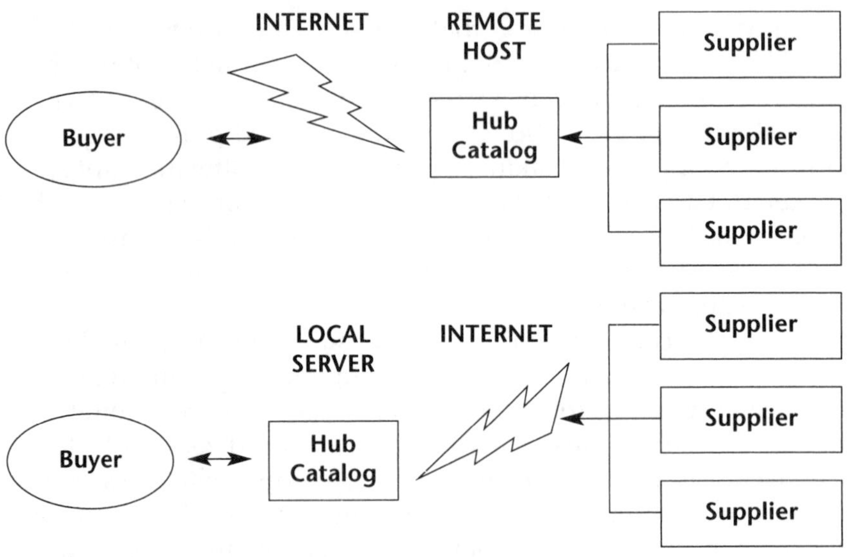

COLLABORATIVE E-PROCUREMENT

E-procurement software is more collaborative than previous generations of procurement technology. It manages electronic collaboration not just with individual suppliers but also with a range of Web buying hubs and online auction sites. (See Exhibit 6.5.)

Buying Hubs

Buying hubs are online marketplaces located on Web servers and reached via the Internet. The spokes to a hub are the community of suppliers who supply content, in the form of products or services, to the hub's online catalog and the customers who use the hub as a gateway to the supplier community.

BEST PRACTICE ACTION ► **IDENTIFY BUYING HUBS.** Identify the buying hubs that make sense for you to participate in either as a customer or as a supplier. Take steps to integrate the hub into your buying process or to make your catalog content available on the hub.

Exhibit 6.5 Collaborative E-Procurement

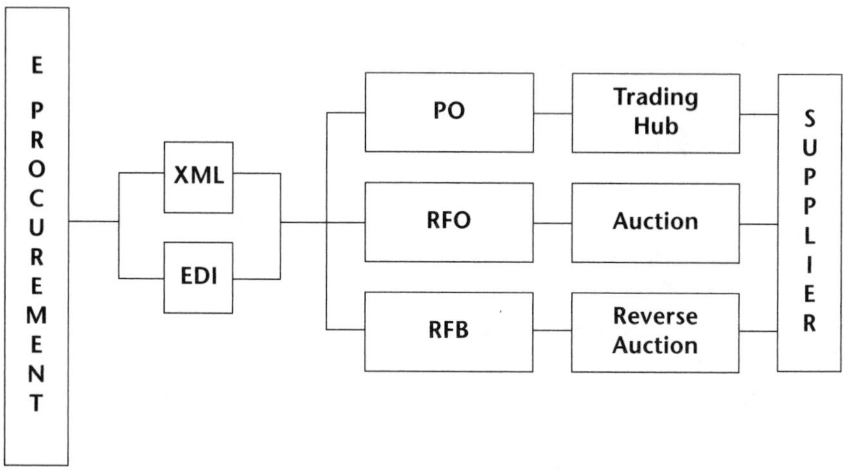

The hub provides either manual or programmatic access to this community of suppliers and their product and/or service catalogs. Manual access is where a user goes to the hub's URL and uses the hub services directly via their Web browser, usually via some sort of portal software. Programmatic access is where an application collaborates directly with the hub using a data interchange mechanism such as traditional EDI messaging or XML-based documents and based on EDI standards such as EDIFACT, X.12, or new Web "standards" such as OBI or RosettaNet.

Broadly speaking, there are two types of trading hubs: horizontal and vertical online malls. A horizontal mall hub offers access to a wide range of diverse suppliers who can service a cross-industry range of product or service requests. A vertical mall has a more narrow and specific supplier community with the aim of servicing a particular industry or delivering specific types of products. A meta-hub, such as VerticalNet, is a hybrid because it operates like a horizontal mall for multiple vertical hubs. Vendors of e-procurement software may operate a trading hub of their own. In such cases, their software is generally tightly integrated with the hub and acts as an on-ramp to the hub from the user desktop. Vendors such as Ariba, CommerceOne, Oracle, and SAP all operate trading hubs for use by customers of their e-procurement software.

Suppliers interact with hubs in at least three ways:

1. They supply product and/or service-related content or links to content for use in the hub's online catalog(s).
2. They respond to request-for-bid documents submitted to the hub by buyers and transmitted to the suppliers electronically.
3. They ship products to the hub customers and update self-service pages or send e-mails to keep customers informed of their order status.

Generally, suppliers pay a fee to the market maker to participate in the trading hub.

Customers (buyers) interact with hubs in at least three ways:

1. They directly access the hub's online product and/or service catalog to browse and order.
2. They complete request-for-bid forms to specify their purchasing requirements and send them electronically to the hub to pass on to appropriate suppliers.
3. They respond to order status information that they receive from suppliers—for example, to cancel an order when they are notified that items are on back order.

Generally, customers do not pay to participate in a trading hub.

Auction Hubs

The suitability of the Internet for matchmaking two remote parties has resulted in the rapid development of online auctions targeted at consumers and pioneered by eBay.com and others. But auctions are not just a consumer-to-consumer activity; they can also support business-to-business (B2B) buying. In this role, the auction process is used to shift distressed inventory in the form of:

- Discontinued product lines
- Surplus inventory
- "Last-minute" spare capacity, such as hotel rooms or air-route seats

There is no practical reason why Internet auctions cannot become a standard source for the procurement of business products and services, alongside more conventional procurement sources (i.e., individual suppliers and trading hubs). There are two main forms of online auctions: conventional and reverse auctions.

A conventional auction essentially sells products or services to the highest bidder, and the process involves matching offers to bids. E-procurement software has to be able to create a request for offer (RFO) and then transmit it programmatically to an online auction hub to determine if what the customer wants is currently on auction. If it is, the software must apply bid-specific business rules to enable the customer to participate in the bidding process until the bid is either won or lost.

Reverse auctions are where suppliers respond by bidding for a customer's business; the process is reversed because it is the buyer who makes the offer and the seller who makes the bids. The e-procurement software initiates a reverse auction by creating a request-for-bid (RFB) document and transmitting it programmatically to the reverse auction hub. Hub suppliers respond to the RFB with their own bids for the customer's business either via an e-mail message or programmatically so that the customer can review and compare all the bids via a self-service page not accessible to the bidding suppliers. The customer can then select (or discard) the bids based on the price, terms, delivery, and so on.

More and more conventional trading hubs on the Web, such as Mondus, are beginning to offer access to auctions as another complementary procurement source for their community of buyers and as a means to increase their community of suppliers.

E-procurement technology is dramatically changing the way that employees participate in the procurement process, reengineering the role of the purchasing department, and expanding the range of options available to source suppliers and buy products. More efficient procurement generally leads to real bottom-line costs savings and enables e-businesses to reduce the number of staff involved in what is, in most businesses, a non–value-added process and administrative burden.

CHAPTER SEVEN

Knowledge Management

Arguably, e-businesses have three key assets: their people, partners, and technology. But these assets in turn depend on another, intangible asset—namely knowledge. Lacking brick-and-mortar assets, "pure" e-businesses function effectively because their people benefit from superior business process, technology, partnering, and marketplace knowledge. Consequently, in the e-business world, knowledge assumes even greater importance because its existence actually drives the business—it is a "mission-critical" asset and one that is impossible to outsource.

But because knowledge is generally regarded as an intangible asset (except for specific tangible knowledge assets, such as patents or book copyrights) some businesses fail to pay knowledge same degree of attention that they pay to tangible assets such as plant, property, and equipment. It seems incredible, but in many businesses is it easier to find out the location of an individual PC and its net present value through a fixed asset management package than it is to understand the breadth and depth of the company knowledge assets and how to get hold of knowledge.

Enlightened e-business managers cannot allow this to occur in their organizations. They understand the asset value of knowledge and its potential to "turn information and data into effective action," as advocated by the authors of *Managing Knowledge* (Addison-Wesley, 1999). These managers also know that knowledge management (KM) introduces a number of challenges, including:

- Managing data quantity
- Managing information quality

- Acquiring, synthesizing, and disseminating knowledge
- Enhancing the knowledge asset value of the organization

Knowledge sits at the top of a pyramid. (See Exhibit 7.1.) The only way to manage it effectively is to understand how to source, organize, and disseminate knowledge within and outside of an organization. Sourcing knowledge depends on spreading as wide a net as possible to find the data sources that provide the raw material for knowledge acquisition. Organizing knowledge means creating the information warehouses that aggregate or categorize data and put it into a format suitable for knowledge acquisition. Knowledge acquisition, synthesis, and dissemination depends on the use of specific technology tools that "mine" these information warehouses for knowledge, make some kind of decision, and communicate the results to the individuals or systems that can "action" these decisions. Finally, KM is not just about leveraging what you know already; it also is about proactively enhancing corporate knowledge.

The following acronyms and terms are used in this chapter.

TERM	DESCRIPTION
Data source	File system or database where data is stored and accessed from
Domain	Area of expertise relevant to knowledge management
Domain expert	Person or Web site with expertise relating to a specific domain
EDM	Electronic document management
E-learning	Distance learning over the Internet
KM	Knowledge management
Reportal	Web-based report organization and viewing software
Warehouse	A database storing a collection of aggregated and/or categorized data

Exhibit 7.1 Knowledge Pyramid

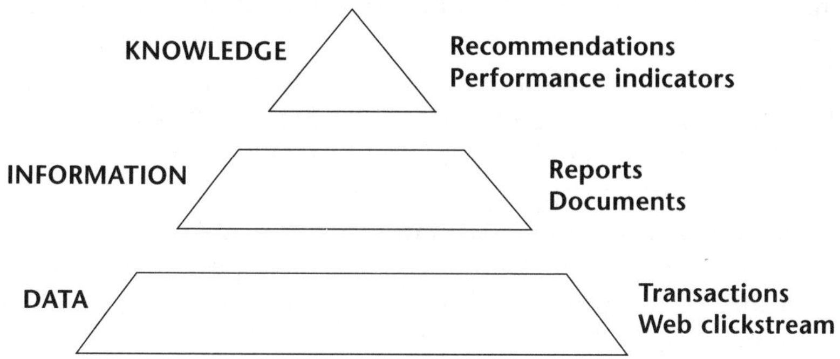

THE KM LANDSCAPE

Any KM initiative must begin by recognizing the differences among data, information, and knowledge. (See Exhibit 7.1.) In today's organizations:

- Data consists of entities such as transactions and clickstreams represented by rows in database tables and data in Web server log files
- Information is represented by entities such as documents and reports that organize data into recognizable formats that communicate information from the data—for example, the document and worksheet files created by word processing and spreadsheet software or generated from the document formatters and report writers found in transaction processing systems handling ERP or CRM.
- Knowledge is represented by entities such as alerts, key performance indicators, and visual charts that depend on both individual and contextual analysis of information sources, and by human expertise gathered from years of experience

This data, information, and knowledge is one aspect of the organizational landscape that benefits from regular surveying to divide it up into domains—areas of focus that combine electronic data and information repositories with human domain experts. A domain expert is an individual located either within a company or externally who is a source for specific domain knowledge—such as an internal business analyst or an external industry analyst. A domain may encompass domain experts, business process work flows, and a wide variety of local or remote file systems, databases, and Web sites.

These domains could have an internal or external focus. An internal focus might be on product, customer, supplier, or employee. An external focus might be on territory, industry, political, or competitive landscape.

Naturally, these domains cannot be managed successfully through the use of internal resources alone, as shown by the overview of a customer domain in Exhibit 7.2. Every business depends more or less on external knowledge sources, such as university research departments, industry analyst groups, market research firms, and others, for effective management of their knowledge domains.

Once these domains have been classified, it is more important to identify domain-specific data sources, information warehouses,

Exhibit 7.2 The Customer Domain

INTERNAL SOURCES	CUSTOMER DOMAIN	EXTERNAL SOURCES

Internal	External
Repositories	**Repositories**
• CRM system	• Libraries
• ERP system	• TV, radio, video
• Web storefront	• Web sites
Experts	**Experts**
• Delivery people	• Academics
• Salespeople	• Consultants
• Service people	• Industry analysts

BEST PRACTICE ACTION ► **EXPOSE YOUR EXPERTS.** Many corporate intranets contain pages with links to other Web sites where specific information can be found. But does your intranet include e-mail links to a categorized list of domain experts both within and outside your organization who are willing and able to deliver specific expertise to your employees?

and domain experts than to attempt to focus effort on knowledge capture from specific domain experts.

The knowledge landscape also includes the people and systems who participate in the process of KM, including:

- Knowledge generators
- Knowledge analysts
- Knowledge consumers

Part of the first steps of any KM initiative must be to define and rank, in terms of their level of knowledge value added, these participants in the knowledge process. Knowledge generators are the people (called domain experts earlier) and systems that have the potential to generate knowledge useful to the business. Knowledge analysts are people and systems that can take the output of knowledge generators and help make sure it reaches the right knowledge consumers in useful formats. Knowledge consumers are generally people (rather than systems) who need to use knowledge to perform their organizational roles more effectively. All these people exist in every organization today; is it just that this role has been largely unrecognized until recently.

BEST PRACTICE ACTION ► **PROFILE KNOWLEDGE PARTICIPANTS.** Categorize, list, and rank the participants (people and systems) in your knowledge process. Profile each classification of participant in terms of its knowledge role: How and what kind of knowledge do they generate, analyze, or consume?

DATA SOURCES

Knowledge management depends on the ability to properly manage the lowest level of the knowledge pyramid, namely data management, by minimizing offline data and centralizing data control.

Offline data management is anathema to KM, since data can escape the net of any KM technology. It is difficult to prevent domain experts from keeping knowledge in their heads, but e-business managers can at least ensure that every business transaction and every business document is captured electronically. Three important transactions capture systems likely to play an important role as data sources for knowledge acquisition include ERP, CRM, and Web site/storefront clickstream log files. Other knowledge capture systems include imaging systems, video cameras, voice recorders, and electronic content management software, used to create electronic files from various types of source data, and then index and organize these files for easier access.

Besides bringing data and its management online, another key aspect of data management is storing it in a limited number of centralized online data sources. Localized transaction and document management, at the desktop rather than at the network server level, creates information islands that also can escape the KM net. The use of shared database, network, and Web servers, rather than local hard disks, personal data files, and Web servers, to store documents and transactions ensures that data is centralized rather than localized and accessible to many rather than to few employees.

By eliminating offline data and centralizing its storage, you create a discrete set of data sources that represent a foundation

BEST PRACTICE ACTION ► ELIMINATE OFFLINE DATA. Perform a data management gap analysis to determine what, if any, data is being managed offline and whether significant amounts of useful data is being stored locally rather than on centralized database, network, and Web servers. The results of this gap analysis represents holes in your overall ability to manage your organizational knowledge that should be plugged by better overall corporate data management policies.

from which information and then knowledge can be derived. There are two primary types of data store:

1. Unstructured data—in the form of files such as image, text, and voice files
2. Structured data—in the form of database tables or XML documents

Heterogeneous file systems and databases may well be found within an organization, together with Web sites that act as a repository for both structured and unstructured data sources, that are often located outside organizational boundaries and controlled by a third party. In larger organizations it is a challenge simply to keep up with the ever-changing data source landscape and changing organizational boundaries. This is just one reason why cross-departmental roles, such as chief knowledge officer (CKO), are being introduced and backed up by staff focused specifically on delivering enterprise-wide KM.

Smaller businesses that cannot afford specific KM-focused resources should at the least provide a means to maintain an up-to-date list of data sources, Web sites, and domain experts available to employees through an existing shared resource such as the corporate intranet or employee portal.

INFORMATION WAREHOUSES

Once the domains and their data repository data sources have been defined and identified, the next task is to ensure that data gets organized into appropriate information warehouses or libraries, as shown in Exhibit 7.3. These information repositories form a middle tier between the back-end data sources and the knowledge-generation front-end tools that actually deliver knowledge to the user.

Each warehouse consolidates data of a specific type, puts it in a format suitable for knowledge-generating tools to work with, and organizes it according to some kind of structure. Exhibit 7.4 lists these warehouses.

Exhibit 7.3 Data Sources and Information Warehouses

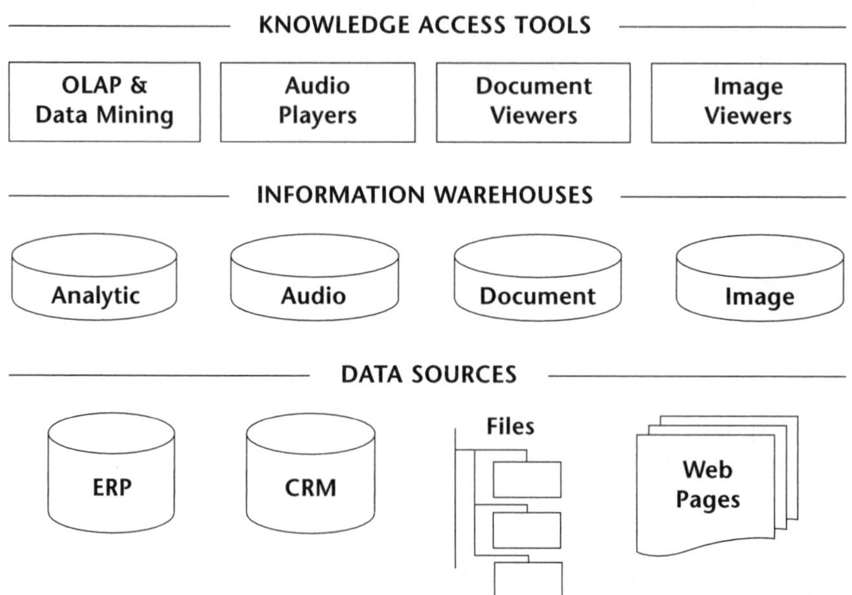

All these warehouses could be supported by a single server computer running a universal database engine capable of handling the storage and management of the various data types (text, image, sound, video, etc.) needed. But it is more likely that these warehouses use their own dedicated server computer and database, something that adds complexity to the IT management of the technology infrastructure required to support KM within an organization.

The organizational structure of these repositories is what changes data into information because it changes the nature of the incoming data (e.g., by aggregating transaction data into summary data) or because it associates the data with structured categorization criteria, such as information dimensions, hierarchies, or keywords. In most businesses KM is likely to depend on at least two information warehouses being available, the analytic warehouse (usually known as a data warehouse or data mart) and the document or report library.

Besides internal information repositories, external information repositories may need to be monitored. For example, a company

Exhibit 7.4 Knowledge Warehouse Types

Warehouse	*Format*	*Organization*
Analytic	Summarized transaction data suitable for use by online analytical processing and data mining tools	By territory, product, customer
Audio	Audio clips and tracks suitable for playing through a speaker system or recording to a removable removable format such as a CD	By topic, band, project
Document	Repositories of document and report files that can be viewed on screen, printed, or converted to other file formats	By topic, department, company, author
Image	Image or video files than can be viewed on screen or transferred to DVD or CD media, for example	By topic, geography, product

may choose to monitor a competitor's public Web site or other infomediary Web sites that aggregate information, such as news from around the world or patent applications received and approved.

BEST PRACTICE ACTION ➤ **ENCOMPASS EXTERNAL EXPERTISE.** When identifying and creating your information repositories, do not forget to identify external information repositories that need regular monitoring to play their part in the knowledge synthesis process. Remember that this type of monitoring will require specialist software to be effective, not simply the subscribe-to-site type of functionality found in most Web browsers today.

DISSEMINATING KNOWLEDGE

The information warehouses provide the starting point for knowledge dissemination that consists of

- Synthesizing knowledge
- Triggering knowledge events
- Communicating knowledge

Knowledge synthesis may depend on manual discovery of knowledge (e.g., through the use of desktop online analytical processing (OLAP) tools) by business analysts working with data in analytic warehouse. Or it may be wholly or partially automated in that knowledge is exposed via more the more specialized tools used for data mining, contextual analysis, performance scorecarding, or business alert generation.

In each case these tools depend on the definition of business rules that they can utilize to make decisions about whether the information they are synthesizing creates knowledge. If so, is a knowledge event triggered that someone in the organization needs to know about? A knowledge event is simply an event that has a knowledge-related impact; it could be generated by a database management system, a business process work-flow management system, or an individual's flash of inspiration.

> **BEST PRACTICE ACTION** ► **EVENT-DRIVEN KM.** The best way to build your KM foundation may be to identify key knowledge events first and then work backward from these event definitions to determine the information warehouse(s) and data source(s) required to support the exposure of these knowledge events.

Once a knowledge event is triggered, the knowledge must be communicated to people who can take advantage of (or "action") this knowledge. (See Exhibit 7.5.) These people could be internal employees or external business partners who are "subscribed" to this knowledge event and who are earmarked to receive some sort of electronic notification of it.

Each knowledge event will service different subscriber groups and deliver a different package to them. The range of packages could include generating

- A document, report chart, or worksheet to illuminate the event
- An e-mail message with or without attachment
- An alert that shows up in an employee Web portal
- A to-do item that shows up in an employee work-flow in box

Exhibit 7.5 Knowledge Event Work Flow

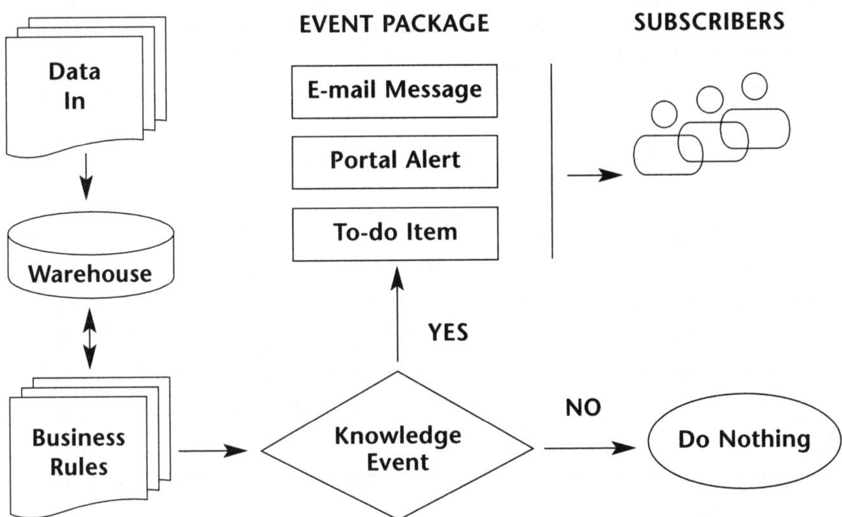

A single knowledge event could require action packages to be sent to more than one subscriber group in more than one format, depending on the event and the individual recipient's organizational role.

Disseminating knowledge requires a three-step process to: (1) identify a knowledge event, (2) define the target subscribers, and (3) determine the right package to send them to communicate the knowledge as effectively as possible.

Knowledge Event	*Subscribers*	*Package*
Internal Event		
New product released	Sales and service	E-mail URL link to product specifications and price list
Fraud pattern detected on Web storefront	Payment service provider	E-mail alert with report attachment for follow-up
External Event		
Competitor makes acquisition	Product managers	Portal alert with URL link to competitor's press release
New patent registered	Research and development	To-do item with URL link to patent description

> **BEST PRACTICE ACTION ► THE KNOWLEDGE DELIVERY CHAIN.** Figure out your knowledge delivery chain by defining knowledge events, mapping them to subscriber groups, and determining the right way to communicate the knowledge to individuals within these groups.

Knowledge dissemination is unlikely to succeed if it depends on armies of staff, personally searching to uncover knowledge events and creating and dispatching the action packages. Knowledge dissemination also should be occurring on a daily basis in response to a wide range of internal and external events and data. Such knowledge dissemination can be managed only with technology. It depends on a foundation infrastructure of data sources and information warehouses, the organizational knowledge base, being in place first.

ENHANCING KNOWLEDGE

Because knowledge is an asset, it must be continuously enhanced to ensure that its asset value is maintained in the face of a rapidly changing knowledge environment. Knowledge enhancement is about updating and adding to employee and corporate knowledge on a regular basis. It means:

- Adding new data sources and information warehouses as a new knowledge need is identified
- Constantly refining the business rules associated with knowledge events and identifying new events as business processes change
- Updating the profiles of knowledge participants to make sure that their value added to the organization is always focused in the right areas
- Rolling out Web-based e-learning to knowledge participants to broaden or deepen their knowledge within existing or new domains

Knowledge management must be a proactive and ongoing process to succeed; "stale" knowledge is a contradiction in terms and is useless in the fast-moving world of e-business.

KNOWLEDGE TECHNOLOGY

As Exhibit 7.6 shows, there is no such thing as a single product that can encompass all the needs of KM. A KM system comprises many different technologies that together have the potential to deliver and manage knowledge.

Whereas data warehouses, electronic document libraries, and data mining tools may have been key KM technologies in the past, the future is likely to focus on different technologies, including the use of

- Web-based corporate portals as the primary means for disseminating knowledge generally and specifically as a way for

Exhibit 7.6 Knowledge Management System

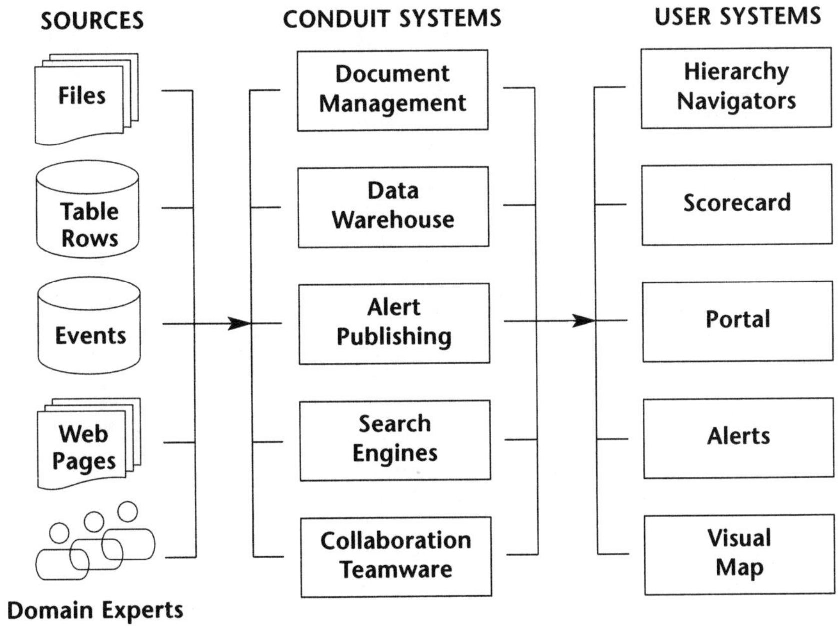

individual domain experts to make their knowledge accessible through their own subportals

- Event-monitoring and contextual data analysis tools to identify knowledge events and push them out to knowledge analysts
- Performance dashboards that can communicate knowledge in a visual and easy-to-assimilate way to knowledge consumers and personalization tools that make it easier for consumers to subscribe to knowledge channels
- Search engines that use XML-structured source data, either in documents or databases, to allow more wide-ranging and powerful searches across internal and external information warehouses and Web sites

Knowledge management has to be a core competency of e-businesses. If it is not, they are likely quickly to lose their competitive edge in a business environment where knowledge assets may be more important than physical assets.

CHAPTER EIGHT

Digital Asset Management

E-businesses are likely to have to manage more digital assets than ever before simply because more things are being managed digitally—documents, reports, messages, transactions, and so on. Aiming for best practice in digital asset management is fast becoming another skill e-business managers need to master. This chapter focuses on two specific aspects of digital asset management, providing access to digital assets and message management.

Providing access to digital assets concerns the use of portal technology to provide a gateway to those assets. Message management deals with managing the increasing volume and influence of electronic mail in business life. Web content management covers the organizational structures needed to manage the face of an organization on the Internet.

The following terms are used in this chapter.

TERM	DESCRIPTION
Content	Documents, reports, news feeds, graphics, and the like viewed on Web sites
DRM	Digital rights management
Firewall	Software to protect systems from unauthorized access via the Internet
Portal	A Web-based gateway to people, processes, systems, and content

TERM	DESCRIPTION *(continued)*
Portlet	A discrete "applet" that delivers functions and/or content within a portal
Personalization	Customizing a deliverable to the needs of an individual
Reportal	Software used to organize and view reports over the Internet
Teamware	Software focused on supporting collaborative activities over the Internet

PORTALS: GATEWAYS TO DIGITAL ASSETS

The short history of portals begins with Internet search engines. Several years ago, as the search-engine business became more competitive, providers like Yahoo! began to surround their core search engines with other content and links to make their sites more attractive to visitors. The idea was that Web surfers would make a specific site their "portal"—a gateway or on-ramp to the Internet. Portals were focused on delivering a wide range of content links and a community feel to encourage users to stick with a single portal as their own homepage on the Internet.

Since that time Web portals aimed at consumers have become more sophisticated. Now they link consumers to third-party Web services through affiliate partnerships and allow users to customize the portal so it becomes more personalized to their needs—the "MyPortal" approach.

The portal concept is now being applied to digital asset management within organizations, as a means to create "corporate" portals—Web-based gateways to the people, processes, systems, and content managed within or relevant to a specific corporation. In effect, a portal becomes the digital front end or face of the organization to the world and a primary means of reaching the corporate digital and human assets. (See Exhibit 8.1.)

In every corporation, at least three types of stakeholders should have access to digital and human assets via a portal. These stakeholders include:

1. Internal employees
2. External business partners
3. The general public

The employee portal is often called an intranet. The portal for external business partners is often referred to as an extranet. The portal for the general public is simply the corporate Web site, xyz.com. The difference between these portals hinges simply on security of access and the range of human and digital assets accessible through them. Publicly accessible portals, such as the corporate Web site, offer the least access to corporate knowledge assets and business management systems. Business partner portals typically operate behind a firewall that restricts who can access the portal and when, but offer more access to corporate knowledge and the capability to participate in business processes involving access to internal systems. Employee portals offer the most access to internal knowledge and systems, often acting as a

Exhibit 8.1 Portals: Gateway to Corporate Digital and Human Assets

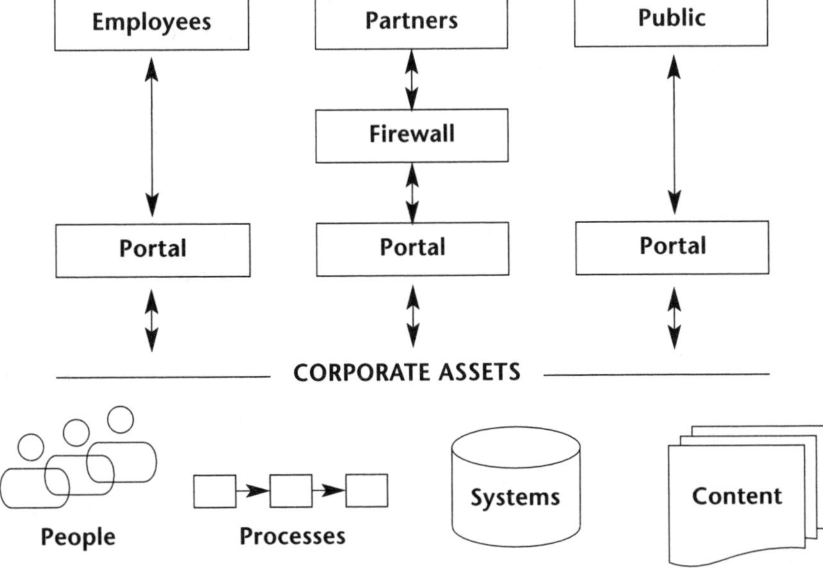

means to present a holistic, integrated view of knowledge and system assets.

BEST PRACTICE ACTION ► PREVENT A PLETHORA OF PORTALS. Think about whether you could use a single technology package or platform to run all three of the main types of portal required by every e-business: employee, partner, and public portals. Although many of today's portal packages are costly, the administrative savings from using a single technology to create and maintain all three portals could cost-justify the technology acquisition.

PORTAL VARIANTS

Creating portals is not just a case of servicing these three main stakeholder communities. Variants of each portal may be required to service different devices, flex to the employee role, and accommodate varying levels of user context or even the temporal aspects of a typical workday.

For example, a portal accessed from within a regular Web browser on a desktop PC must look and behave substantially differently from the same portal running within a microbrowser on a mobile phone. This portal will likely require different technology to build and certainly a fundamentally different design to deliver functions and information effectively to the user.

Employee roles have an important impact on portals that front-end corporate intranets. For example, the portal may support a generic role, such as "employee," to provide every employee with access to general corporate content and collaborative tools such as e-mail, contact databases, and appointment calendars. But in addition, the portal may be required to support specific roles, such as salesperson or manager. Clearly salespeople and managers will need access to additional functions and content, such as order entry and competitor information or expense report approval and departmental or corporate financial statements.

Portals exist to deliver access to functions and information, but the range of functions and information that portals deliver also

> **BEST PRACTICE ACTION ► CUT CONTENT CANNIBALIZATION.** If you are making internal content available via a portal remember to protect specific text, images, sound, and video using digital rights management software (DRM) to prevent your content being misused either by consumers or competitors. DRM software is used to add a protective wrapper to selected pieces of content—such as a digital watermark behind an image for example—that helps to prevent content being copied, printed, or edited without your permission.

depends on the range of contexts the portals have to serve. (See Exhibit 8.2.) A single portal may be required to reflect how the user participates in multidimensional contexts as

- An individual
- A member of a team or department
- An employee located in a particular facility
- A member of an organization
- A participant in supply chains involving external business partners

Exhibit 8.2 Portal Context Onion

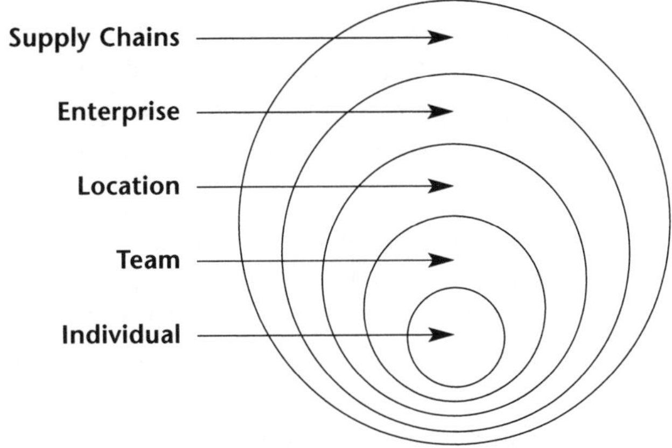

A portal also could be subject to a temporal dimension that helps it reflect an employee's workday more effectively. Different functions or content may be displayed at different times of the day to reflect different temporal needs or even moods, as suggested in Exhibit 8.3.

BEST PRACTICE ACTION ► **CORPORATE PORTALS.** A corporate portal is not just a bunch of content links, news feeds, and stock tickers. Figure out the contexts you want the portal to service and how this impacts the range of functions and information the portal delivers. Increase the relevance of your portal by making it more sensitive to users' daily workday rhythms.

DEPARTMENTAL PORTALS

While the ideal portal might be one that is device, context, and time sensitive, for many organizations a basic departmental portal may be the practical compromise. For example, a portal designed for the finance department might provide Web-based access to

- Selected functions within the corporate ERP system
- Spreadsheet templates, tax forms, or accounting procedure manuals
- A live company stock feed and finance-related news announcements downloaded automatically from a wire service
- Links to Web sites of suppliers, customers, or banking partners for access to their self-service applications
- Links to other Web sites that provide customer credit checking, package shipment tracking, or the latest currency exchange rate feeds
- An electronic in box that managers can access to approve or review transactions, such as time and expense reports, inventory reorder or payment requests, and employee requisitions
- A navigation and search tool that lets users access intranet report libraries to find and view archived financial reports from prior fiscal periods or years

Exhibit 8.3 Portal Deliverables for Times of Day

Time of Day	*Portal Deliverable Highlighted*
Start of Workday	• Today's to-do list and appointments • Thought for the day • Reminder of a historical event • Today's company and competitor news
Lunch Break	• Reading recommendation • Relaxation Web cast • Today's offers from local eateries • Today's news headlines
End of Day	• Recommended movies, shows, events in locality • Music to wind down to • Review of today's achievements • Set next day goals

- A navigation and search tool that lets users access intranet document or image servers to find and view images of invoices, checks, or other financial documents
- Access to the user's regular e-mail in-box
- Pop-up calendars that show corporate events relevant to the finance department
- Business alerts from various line-of-business systems that inform employees about budget overruns, inventory shortages, or new versions of important reports
- Graphical presentation of the status of time and expense reports, requisitions, or payment requests as they progress through their work-flow cycles

Much of the way that functions and content is presented to portal users can be encapsulated within a series of "portlets"—self-contained mini-applications that deliver a specific function or content offering and can be selectively assembled into complete portal pages.

BEST PRACTICE ACTION ► **PORTLETIZE YOUR PORTALS.** Establish a departmental portal template, defining typical functional and information access requirements and leveraging a set of shared portlets. This template and set of portlets can be customized for use across every department to provide a consistent and reusable set of portal building tools.

BUSINESS PARTNER PORTALS

Whereas departmental portals are likely to have a balance of content, commerce, and community, business partner portals are likely to be more focused on commerce and depend on self-service access to corporate ERP and CRM systems. Ultimately the purpose of a partner portal is to make it easier for partners to do business with your company. A partner portal should be capable of providing:

- Self-service access to update data partners "own" in your systems, such as address and contact data
- Views on data relating specifically to their relationship with your company, such as current credit status, open invoices, and orders or payments due
- The ability to query supply chain-related systems for data such as inventory status, inventory demand forecasts, and inventory available to promise
- Documents relating to project or procurement bids for use by suppliers and updated price lists and product configuration tools for use by customers

It is not hard to see how the sophistication of corporate portals will become a competitive weapon for e-businesses. Employees are more likely to want to work for businesses with portals that are context, role, and time sensitive because by using them they will be more effective in their jobs. And business partners are more likely to be interested in working with businesses accessible via a commerce-focused portal that facilitates maintaining a closer partner relationship and delivering a more visible supply chain.

MESSAGE MANAGEMENT

In mid-1999 a Pitney Bowes survey found U.S. workers reporting that they send and receive 201 messages per day, a 6 percent increase over the previous year. The Gartner Group tells us that the volume of e-mail is set to double every year up to the year 2002. That is why message management is fast becoming a critical strategic concern for businesses that want to improve employee productivity, service their prospects and customers more effectively, and avoid costly legal liabilities. If you think of e-mail as a business utility, just like, say, electricity, then it is easy to understand three key areas of message management: (1) safety, (2) metering, and (3) routing.

Message Safety

E-businesses can expect to use e-mail for a wide range of purposes, including:

- Employee-to-employee messaging
- Employee-to-partner messaging
- Employee-to-public messaging
- System-to-system EDI

The messages carried may be of an open and informational nature or of a closed and sensitive nature. But in either case, if a business regularly receives or sends "unsafe" messages or sends and loses messages, it could play havoc with productivity, damage the business's reputation or goodwill, and even trigger unwanted legal action. For example, in the year 2000 the "I Love You" virus transmitted by e-mail caused havoc worldwide, shutting down not just many corporate messaging systems but some entire corporate networks. And e-mail has been used as evidence in court cases, such as the recent high-profile U.S. Department of Justice case against Microsoft. Sending and receiving messages safely should be the first concern of any e-business focused on message management. E-mail travels fast and can damage both the sender and the receiver if not managed safely using message filtering and security tools.

BEST PRACTICE ACTION ➤ **MESSAGES MATTER.** Appoint a message manager, someone with the responsibility for monitoring and managing message traffic, to ensure that messaging systems are being used productively and that the business is not exposing itself to legal or reputation damage, through its e-mail system.

An important task of message filtering is rejecting messages before they even reach you or your business partners. Clearly messages that contain potential viruses must be turned back before they reach corporate servers inside the firewall. So message-by-message virus checking is essential. But now that e-mail has become another way to push advertising, every employee with an e-mail address becomes a target for spam, e-junk mail, which consists of unwanted, time-wasting solicitations. Most desktop e-mail inbox software, such as Eudora Mail or Microsoft Outlook, lets individuals set up antispam filters or blocked sender lists to prevent messages even reaching their inbox. But professional message managers need tools that allow them to enforce a more sophisticated corporate-wide message filtering policy.

These filtering tools act as an intermediary gateway between your internal mail server and the Internet and focus on managing inbound and outbound e-mail. Inbound and outbound message traffic can be checked for viruses, for inappropriate content (e.g., pornographic images), and for approved sender or recipient addresses and can be intercepted if necessary. Inbound messages can be replied to automatically using an autoresponder message such as "Remove me from your list." Outbound messages can have an automatic legal disclaimer, such as confidentiality or copyright notification, attached before they are sent. These e-mail sentinel tools are an important part of the message manager's defensive armory.

Enhanced message security is required when sending time-critical or sensitive-content messages. Merely encrypting the message content, which many desktop e-mail send functions can do, is not enough. The message manager wants to be sure that the message is received by the intended recipient without being intercepted en route. Third-party Web services that receive, secure, route, and track messages via the Internet provide this type of message security.

To use these services, the business registers with the service provider's Web site and creates and sends the message using self-service applets on that site. The message content is checked, encrypted, and stored on the third-party's secure Web server, complete with a unique tracking number. The message recipient is sent an e-mail notifying him or her of the awaiting message. This e-mail includes an embedded URL to click to access the message. When the recipient opens and views the message via the URL link, the sender is sent an e-mail to confirm that the intended recipient received the message. These services also may trap "attack" attempts on the message content by Internet hackers, notifying senders of the attempted hack and rendering the content indecipherable if such attacks take place.

Safe message management ensures that employees are not sending or receiving unproductive or potentially litigious messages and that sensitive content is sent securely with ironclad tracking and destruction in the event of compromise.

BEST PRACTICE ACTION ► **ISOLATE SENSITIVE MESSAGES.** Identify specific messages in your business that could benefit from being handled via a secure messaging service. Determine whether the potential damage resulting from these messages being compromised can cost-justify this type of messaging insurance.

Message Metering

When electricity comes into your home, you care about when and how much you are using because it costs money. Businesses need to meter e-mail messages for much the same reason. Contrary to popular belief, e-mail is not free; every e-mail message has a cost in terms of employee productivity and network bandwidth usage. You can only hope to get a handle on this cost through the use of message metering tools.

Message metering tools generally work with specific mail server software, such as Microsoft Exchange. The tools use the mail server log files to provide a wide range of management reports about messages to answer questions such as:

- How many Internet or internal e-mail messages were sent or received by user?
- Who might be spamming or receiving too much spam?
- Who is sending or receiving the least or the most mail?

Message metering tools also can be used to analyze message activity to facilitate the charge-back and bill-back of e-mail time and expense either to internal departments or to clients. Message metering is a useful way to identify messaging bottlenecks, pinpoint individuals who need help with reducing their message load, and spot potential abuses of either the e-mail system or corporate Internet connections generally.

BEST PRACTICE ACTION ➤ MINIMIZE MESSAGE OVERLOAD. Message overload is a potential stress on any employee in an e-business. Use message metering to determine if the cause of this stress is organizational or due to an employee's bad habits. Either way, the results of the metering should enable message managers to reduce this stress and make every employee more productive.

Message Routing

You cannot get the benefit of electricity without routing it to a device or an outlet. Similarly, business prospects and customers will not see the benefit of sending e-mail to your business unless their messages are answered effectively within a reasonable time frame. Message routing software makes sure that messages get to the right person for a timely response and contributes to the important role e-mail plays in delivering superior prospect and customer relationship management.

Message routing has become even more important as more Web shopping sites and self-service functions use e-mail as the primary interaction channel with consumers or business partners.

Putting up a new online storefront or self-service Web site can generate a virtual tsunami of e-mail that demands sophisticated routing techniques to handle effectively.

A rash of recent surveys remind us that many businesses respond to e-mail requests slowly, if they respond at all. Over the last few years, e-mail routing software vendor Brightware has sponsored independent testing of corporate responsiveness. In 1999, testing found that while some businesses responded to e-mail within minutes of receipt, others took weeks. E-businesses cannot afford to be perceived as slow respondents to e-mail, just as any business cannot afford to fail to return phone calls regularly.

Using the message address, subject, content, or attachments, message routing tools can send messages to individual recipients for direct action or to shared message queues accessible to service-center work groups. Messages can be responded to automatically via user-defined business rules using a standard auto-response reply. Individuals responding to messages can be assisted, by use of an online knowledge base, to create appropriate answers. Routing tools may include work-flow management capabilities to manage complex message routings or use natural language processing to mine the message content for category or emotional themes that will help determine the appropriate recipient and response.

The e-mail messages of customers or prospects with real problems or displaying clear buying signals need to be routed quickly and accurately to their account manager, a specific service rep, or the salesperson most in need of new leads to meet this month's target. Just having a sales@yourcompany.com mailbox on your Web site dumping messages into some public folder in your e-mail system simply will not cut it anymore.

BEST PRACTICE ACTION ► AUTO-RESPOND TO EVERYTHING. With e-mail it's better to auto-respond than not respond at all. The more e-mail that you can auto-respond to, the more likely it is that senders will at least be reassured that their message was received and is being dealt with in a structured manner. Remember that rejecting and returning messages as well as receiving them are valid auto-responses.

Messages as Knowledge

Message management is not just about message safety, metering, and routing. Every message is also potential source of knowledge. The content of and the attachments to a message may need to be archived intelligently so that they benefit not just the recipient but also the recipient's team or department, or the organization as a whole. Message content archiving requires that messages be

- Interrogated for "knowledge markers" in the content so that the message can be forwarded to other employees to whom it may be of interest or stored in a database catagorized using a standard set of analytical criteria
- Checked for attachments that can be filed into the document management system and again categorized for analytical purposes

Treating messages as potential knowledge sources is particularly important in customer-facing systems. Many messages received from potential or existing customers via Web sites or storefronts represent

- Questions that can be incorporated into frequently asked question (FAQ) pages or databases for recycling to all customers and employees
- Complaints and suggestions that can be used by product groups to drive product improvements and enhancements
- Feedback that can be used to improve the navigation or content on a Web site or storefront to make it more effective or point site managers to cross- and up-selling opportunities
- Real-world observations providing information about competitive practices or pricing that can help the marketing group
- Orders that need to be imported into the ERP system's order processing system for fulfillment

Ignoring the knowledge value in e-mail messages undermines the value of a significant e-business asset.

BEST PRACTICE ACTION ► CONDUCT REGULAR MESSAGE AUDITS. When was the last time you audited the messages you received to uncover knowledge items, identify trends and problems, or update blocked sender lists? Make it a practice to allocate some time every quarter to conduct a message audit simply because it is not good practice to allow message traffic to continue unchecked.

Message Rules

In summary, the basis for good message management is an effective set of business rules, as indicated in Exhibit 8.4. A simplified way to encapsulate these rules is in the three Rs of message receiving and the three Ps of message sending.

Exhibit 8.4 Message Rules

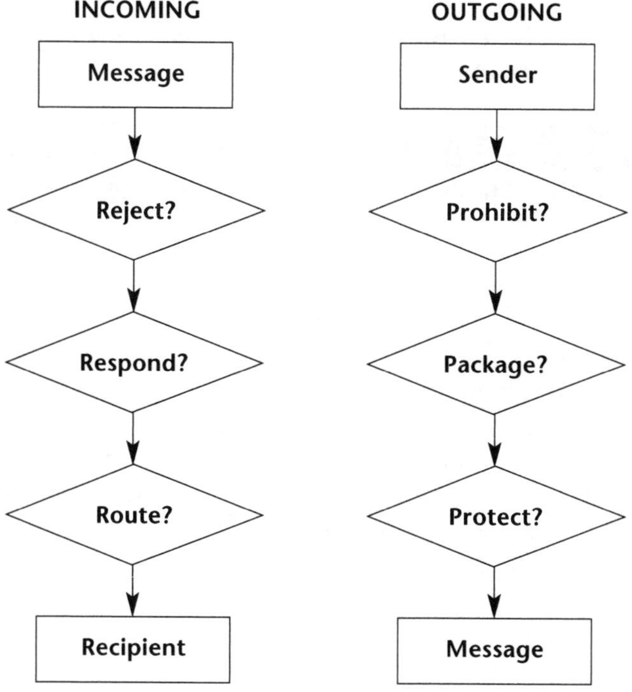

Message receiving rules include whether to:

- **Reject**—because the message has a virus, is from a blocked sender, or contains inappropriate content
- **Respond**—to generate an auto-response based on the sender, recipient, subject, or content of the message
- **Route**—send the message to a specific recipient, or the content to a database, or the attachment to a document management system

Message sending rules include whether to:

- **Prohibit**—block the sending for reasons similar to message rejection above
- **Package**—attach additional content to the message such as a legal disclaimer, confidentiality statement, product offer, or company news release
- **Protect**—encrypt the message based on the sender or recipient or route the message to a Web service for secure message delivery and tracking

BEST PRACTICE ACTION ► **MIND YOUR MESSAGE Rs AND Ps.** If not, identify significant gaps in your message management policy and investigate using rule-based message management technology to plug these gaps.

In many e-businesses, digital asset management involves a great deal more than simply managing access to the assets and message management. But no e-business can avoid the need to make digital assets more accessible via corporate portals or the demands of managing the growing message streams generated by corporate e-mail and EDI-based e-commerce.

CHAPTER NINE

Software as Service

Software as service is not a new concept. In the early days of computing, before packaged software and desktop PCs existed, most businesses had no information technology (IT) resources skilled enough to create software in house. Nor could most afford to acquire and maintain the host computers needed to run the software. Instead, businesses paid to share the processing power and custom-built software on mainframe computers owned either by their bigger business partners or operated by third-party computer bureaus.

In fact, this time-sharing model (based on sharing the processor time) never completely disappeared, despite the arrival of packaged software and ever-cheaper hardware that gave every business the option to bring data processing in house. Many businesses continue to run "administrative" business processes, such as payroll, billing, or payment processing, via an external provider, such as ADP or EDS.

However, this outsourcing of specific, limited business processes does not truly qualify as software as service. Rather it is a means to separate out a processing burden that is a non–value-added activity, such as calculating and generating pay slips or printing and mailing invoices or checks. This type of burden outsourcing has limited and defined input and output, and there is little need for much interactivity in managing the process itself. This is not the same as the emerging software-as-service-paradigm that has been catalyzed by the Internet. Today when it comes to software, every e-business needs to decide whether to build, buy, or broker.

The following acronyms and terms are used in this chapter.

TERM	DESCRIPTION
ASP	Application service provider (on the Internet)
BSP	Business service provider (on the Internet)
Bureau	Third party that maintains host computers for time-sharing use
Deliverable	What a Web service delivers to the service user
ESD	Electronic software distribution
ISP	Internet service provider
Outsourcing	Running business processes or functions at third-party technology sites
Request/Response	Work flow between service user and service provider
Shared services	Consolidating processing at a specific service center site
SLA	Service-level agreement (with ASP, BSP, ISP)
Subscription	Fee paid to subscribe to a service over a period of time
TCO	Total cost of ownership
Time-sharing	Sharing the power of a host processor with other businesses

BUILD, BUY, OR BROKER

In the early days, time-sharing processor power and the software running on those processors meant that most businesses avoided either building or buying software. As hardware costs dropped with the arrival of cheaper mainframe processors and new minicomputers, businesses began buying their own hardware and establishing their own IT departments to build and maintain their business software. But building and maintaining software is a resource-intensive and noncore activity for most businesses. The emergence of packaged software from the 1970s on meant that more businesses could buy business applications off the shelf and limit their building activity to the development of proprietary mission-critical applications that truly deliver competitive edge.

Today's packaged applications are robust and sophisticated enough so that few, if any, businesses would even consider building their own enterprise resource planning (ERP) or customer relationship management) CRM software. But despite the many apparent benefits of buy versus build, the total cost of ownership (TCO) of packaged software remains considerable and tends to be uneven in its distribution. Its cost is front-loaded and spikes each time a new version of the package needs to be installed.

It seems that just as the TCO of packaged applications became an issue, especially for larger corporations with a large and diverse asset base of packaged software, the Internet came along to provide a new alternative: software as service. Internet service providers (ISPs)—organizations running Web servers connected to the Internet—can act as brokers between businesses and the applications they need. Assuming everything else is equal, it is hard to see what the difference is for a user between running an application on a remote network server managed in house on a local or wide area network (LAN or WAN) and running the same application on a remote Web server managed by a service provider over the Internet.

For an e-business, brokering software applications via a service provider has certain attractions, including the ability to:

- Operate an "asset-light" operation because there is less need for software and hardware assets to be bought or leased as these assets are owned by the service provider
- Function with a lower headcount and an IT department focused on adding value because less in-house systems means less administrative burden on IT resources and more flexibility to focus skills on value-added tasks
- Avoid spending scarce start-up funding acquiring hardware and software assets and smooth significant amounts of IT costs over a longer period for improved cash flow
- Increase the flexibility of business managers to respond to rapid technology change by not encumbering them with

costly legacy assets that must be divested regularly to cope with technology churn

These and other benefits to be outlined mean that for e-businesses, today's decision is focused less on whether to build or buy but more on what applications to broker, from whom, and on what basis.

BEST PRACTICE ACTION ► **INSOURCE OR OUTSOURCE?** Undertake an application audit to divide up the applications you use or intend to use into the three categories of build, buy, or broker. For those applications that can be brokered, undertake a further risk assessment by application to determine whether brokering really is a viable option.

For every business, brokering software also involves risks, including:

- A dependence on the Internet from an availability and performance perspective. Just as no packaged software is guaranteed bug-free, no service delivered over the Internet can guarantee that it will not be hacked in to, will be available whenever needed, or will provide a consistent level of performance at all times.
- Transporting your data beyond the firewall: If someone else manages the physical storage of data that you transfer across a public network (the Internet), that data could be compromised, despite all assurances to the contrary.
- Service provider cowboys: Service providing over the Internet is new. Despite appearances to the contrary it is hard to

BEST PRACTICE ACTION ► **A SERVICE PROVIDER IS A KEY SUPPLIER.** If you decide to broker an application, do the right level of "from whom" due diligence. Look at the background of your service provider's management, funding basis, the standing of partners, and the vision and practicality embodied in the choice of technology platform.

manage successfully and profitably. Businesses are at risk from poorly resourced or poorly managed "cowboy" outfits that may not offer the longevity and stability you need.

FROM ISP TO BSP

Initially businesses became involved with the Internet via an Internet service provider. The role of the ISP is to host and manage corporate Web sites and e-mail messaging on servers located on the Web and accessed over the Internet. The ISP provides an essential on-ramp to the Internet for many businesses. As competition increased, many ISPs expanded their offerings to include other services, such as hosting Web storefronts for e-commerce purposes, something that demands a more sophisticated technology infrastructure to support properly.

In the last couple of years we have seen the emergence of the application service provider (ASP), specialist ISPs that take care of hosting and managing one or more business applications, such as an ERP system. The ASP provides both the hardware and the services required to support these more demanding line-of-business applications and rents them out as an Internet service, usually on the basis of a per-user, per-month rental fee.

Now ISPs and ASPs are being joined by the business service providers (BSPs) that deliver electronic access to specific types of business services over the Internet. Unlike ISPs, BSPs do not host corporate Web sites or e-mail servers. And unlike ASPs, BSPs do not host existing packaged applications and rent them to corporations that want to outsource the application functions. Instead, BSPs offer a pure service model. The software they use to deliver the service is not available as a shrink-wrapped product, and the service usually complements the functionality found in a shrink-wrapped product (whether used in-house or hosted via an ASP).

It is certain that, over time, every e-business will need to make use of ISPs, ASPs, and BSPs, since they all perform slightly different tasks. (See Exhibit 9.1.) Although ISPs are an important part of the software as service mix, the e-business infrastructure services they deliver (e.g., site hosting and e-mail) are already a commodity. The sections that follow focus on more on best practice involvement with ASPs and BSPs.

Exhibit 9.1 ISP–ASP–BSP

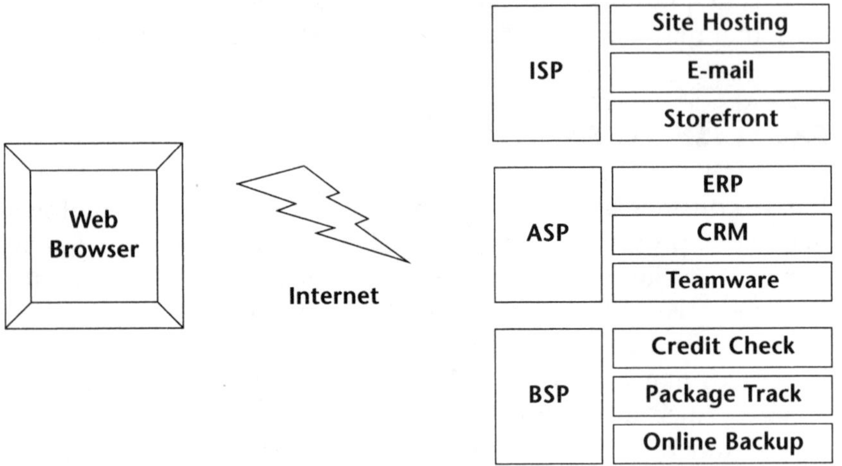

ASPs

Application service providers (ASPs) host one or more packaged applications and make them available for rent to businesses. The rental is generally based on a per-user, per-month fee with price breaks for higher numbers of users and longer contract terms. Generally these packaged applications are the same as the shrink-wrapped product that corporations buy directly from a vendor/reseller to install and use in-house. The software is delivered as a service, but it is important to remember that it was not specifically designed for use in this way. Over time, we can expect that the ASP version of a software package may begin to diverge functionally from the shrink-wrapped version. Eventually it may replace the shrink-wrapped version altogether.

The applications hosted by ASPs do not manage just the "burden" functions of the past but typically support complete business processes and whole functional departments. While initial offerings of ASPs were hosted versions of popular ERP and CRM suites, most recent offerings focus on delivering desktop productivity applications, such as Microsoft Office applications. Typically these applications function the same when used via an ASP Web server as they do when used from an in-house network application server; the only difference is that the application generally runs within a Web browser and does not require a more resource-intensive desktop environment such as Microsoft Windows.

BEST PRACTICE ACTION ► **TRY TEAMWARE FIRST.** Even if ERP or CRM outsourcing via an ASP is not right for your business, an ASP or BSP service may be ideal for implementing "teamware"—applications focused on supporting collaborative activities and geographically dispersed teams such as group calendaring, managing project time and expense, document management, and report distribution and viewing.

Outsourcing an ERP application via an ASP has many obvious benefits for any type and size of business. The ASP maintains the hardware server "farms" required to efficiently host complex applications and removes the need for you to buy, maintain, and upgrade in-house hardware. The ASP can make sure that the latest versions of applications are available to all your users enterprise-wide without the need for costly site-by-site rollouts of new server versions. Using an ASP-based ERP system also means that the only client software required on the user desktop is a Web browser; this eliminates the need to manage client software on a desk-by-desk basis. These three benefits alone could reduce the number of IT people needed to manage an in-house ERP system by one or more full-time equivalents.

But it is not just reductions in IT costs that make ASP outsourcing attractive, it is also other, less tangible benefits. New users or work groups can be signed up for an application almost at a moment's notice, via a Web-based self-service form, without the need for complex infrastructure and implementation-resourcing planning. New users can be given access to the application without worrying about whether their local technology environment needs to be upgraded first. Thus businesses can respond faster to the need to roll out new applications, such as sales force automation or customer relationship management, can bring on more users or users from remote offices faster, or can adapt to merger and acquisition activity more easily.

These benefits of using an ASP can apply to small businesses as much as to geographically dispersed multinationals. The simple pricing model of an outsourced ASP application, usually an initial setup fee plus a monthly rental fee per user, is also very attractive to simplify cash-flow management. This pricing also means that small businesses can make use of big-ticket applications, such as a top-tier ERP suite that they can grow into, that would have been far too costly for them to consider in its shrink-wrapped form. And there is no need to worry about operating system, database, or application user-licensing fees and compliance; the ASP takes care of that by bundling all the license fees within the single monthly fee.

The technology requirements for running an outsourced application over the Internet are relatively straightforward from the perspective of the application user. Depending on the design of the application being outsourced, you should need no in-house application or database servers whatever to support the application. If the ASP is hosting a properly designed browser/server application, nothing more than a Web browser on each device (PC, laptop, handheld, mobile phone, etc.) used to access the application should be needed.

Clearly, every user of the outsourced application needs secure access (via a firewall) to the Internet, preferably a full-time, high-speed connection (such as ISDN/ADSL) using a virtual private network (VPN) connection managed by the ASP. Connectivity to e-mail is also required at the user desktop. This is how the outsourced application delivers reports, documents, and business alerts electronically; facilitates participation in work flows and maintains a support dialogue with individual users. Given that most businesses now have Internet access and e-mail, not much new or even upgraded technology should be required to take advantage of an ASP outsourced application.

However, there are some specific drawbacks to the ASP outsourcing model apart from those generally identified, including:

- A complex system such as an outsourced ERP suite will still require considerable time to configure to your specific business needs. Hosting by an ASP is unlikely to save much application implementation time and effort unless you can accept a completely generic version.
- Integrating an ASP-managed system with complementary systems run in-house, such as an ASP-run CRM system with an in-house ERP system, could prove challenging.

- Not every application available today has either a complete or a well field-tested Web interface. Therefore, its availability to every user could be restricted or using it remotely over the Internet could cause frustrating problems.
- It is likely that using an ASP will make sense only if extensive modifications do not need to be made to a packaged application for your specific needs. The aim of an ASP is to have every customer use the same code base, not the nightmare of managing dozens of different customized versions.
- Many ASPs are only really focused on delivering applications that are suitable for and delivered to corporations operating in North America, so localized or multilingual versions of the application may not be available.

What to Expect from an ASP

- Web site hosting and e-mail store-and-route services
- Configurable e-commerce storefronts for selling on the Web
- Access to procurement trading hubs for buying on the Web
- ERP and other complementary business application hosting
- Availability of dedicated (rather than shared) servers
- Ability to quickly add additional servers for better performance
- Support for EDI or XML-based electronic transaction transmission
- Secure access to application servers over the Internet (e.g., via a VPN)
- Highly configurable application-level security to limit functional access
- Template-based ERP system setup functions to reduce implementation time
- Online application training courses, manuals, and frequently asked questions (FAQs)
- Online application support via real-time Internet chat, e-mail, and self-service help desks

- 24/7/365 application uptime by providing redundant "fail-over" servers as backup
- Automated offline data backup scheduling for disaster recovery
- A fully secured, fireproofed physical server farm facility

BEST PRACTICE ACTION ► QUESTIONS TO ASK YOUR ASP

- ► What database is used to store your application data? Is there a choice?
- ► What server operating system is used to run the servers? Is there a choice?
- ► What technology partnerships does the ASP participate in?
- ► How fast is the ASP's own connection to the Internet?
- ► Is any technology required at your desktop other than a Web browser? Is only a Wintel browser supported?
- ► Who provides first-line support for the application: the ASP or the vendor?
- ► Are there any limits on numbers of transactions, reports, documents, and so on?
- ► Does the ASP provide implementation and training services? If not, who does?
- ► How does the ASP manage the application software upgrade process?
- ► How regularly do the ASP's systems back up data?
- ► Where is the ASP's server farm facility, and can it be inspected?
- ► Can the application be customized in any way?
- ► Is the application available in country-specific (localized) versions?
- ► Who owns the software license: you or the ASP?
- ► Are you renting the application or renting to buy?
- ► Does the ASP provide usage statistics on a self-service basis?

- Automatic load balancing to ensure optimum application accessibility under user load
- Simple "add a new user" Web sign-up for easy acceptance of new users
- User-based monthly application rental fee and low (if any) initial system setup fee
- Regular statistics showing user activity by application for usage analysis
- Delivery of application reports, documents, alerts to users via e-mail
- Participation in electronic work flows via e-mail or a Web browser
- Service-level agreements to ensure mutually acceptable service standards are met
- Automated facilities for the upload and download of data to and from applications
- Automated import capabilities to speed up the data acquisition process
- Partnerships with other ASPs to facilitate application data sharing/passing

BSPs

A BSP does not host a shrink-wrapped application and rent it out. A BSP delivers a service over the Internet that usually complements or enhances the functionality of an in-house or ASP-hosted application. The Internet currently supports many types of BSPs. Many types of e-commerce Web sites, such as trading hubs or auction sites, are really nothing more than BSPs. Exhibit 9.2 shows some of the main types of BSP that exist today and what kind of service they provide.

A content provider supplies content that businesses can use to distribute on their own intranets or via their own corporate portals. News feeds are a common type of content required on corporate intranets and portals. Dozens of BSPs can deliver these

Exhibit 9.2 BSP Types and Services

Type	*Service Example*
Content Provider	BSP that provides news headlines to a Web site
Commerce Enabler	BSP that helps you buy or sell over the Internet
IT Outsourcing	BSP that delivers outsourced IT services
Process Enhancer	BSP that adds value to a specific business process

feeds in various ways. Other examples of content providing include articles supplied by online publications or alerts supplied by registration bodies (e.g., to alert you to a new patent application or bankruptcy relevant to your line of business).

A commerce enabler provides a service that helps your business participate in collaborative supply chains with other businesses with which you may otherwise have no formal or "trusted" business relationship. Trading hubs that let you buy from or sell to their communities of suppliers or customers are the most obvious examples of this type of BSP.

An outsourced IT service provider is a BSP providing a service that reduces a business's reliance on its internal IT resources. Online backup, where you regularly back up selected files to a remote and secure server on the Internet, is a good example of outsourcing a task that is typically managed by internal IT people. You could back up files before there was an Internet and even back them up to a remote server, but no easy and cheap remote service was available to outsource this task to a third party until the Internet was available.

A process enhancement service is a BSP offering that adds value to a specific business process. For example, a banking BSP can help with cash management by providing transactions electronically to facilitate the statement reconciliation process in a general ledger or cash management module. Or a shipping BSP can help with supply chain management by providing shipment rate comparison or real-time shipment tracking services to an order processing or Web storefront module.

Of all the types of BSP outlined, the process enhancement type is certain to have the most significant impact on the widest range of businesses and to add most value to existing packaged applications that run in house.

What to Expect from a BSP

A BSP runs Web and application servers that are connected to the Internet and designed specifically to respond to service requests. Typically, BSP services are accessed via a URL, operate in request-response mode based on manual (direct) input via a Web portal or programmatic control, and use an XML-based application programming interface (API).

When a service operates in request-response mode, you must provide it with some information (a request) in order for it to deliver the service (the response). A service responds by delivering the information you requested on-screen, via an e-mail message, or in some other way, such as in the form of a file you can download to your local desktop PC or application server.

Direct access means that a user goes to the BSP site directly and fills in one or more self-service request forms to specify a service request. (Usually the user must register with the BSP first.) Since direct access typically caters to the one-time user, the BSP is likely to charge for this service delivery via a one-time credit card charge.

Programmatic access means that an in-house (or outsourced) application program communicates and collaborates directly with the BSP application to make the service request and manage the receiving and management of the response. In this case the service user probably has a subscription agreement with the BSP to allow for multiple use of the service.

The use of XML to manage the request and response process is already common among BSPs for accessing their services programmatically over the Internet. As the use of XML becomes more pervasive in business applications, connecting existing shrink-wrapped applications to BSPs using standard request-response schemas, will become easier. These schemas are the type of deliverable resulting from current XML initiatives, such as Microsoft BizTalk. Every module of an ERP system, for example, probably includes opportunities to use BSPs to add value by enhancing the way a business process is managed. (See Exhibit 9.3.)

Of course, the use of BSP services depends on the ability of the application to hook into the BSP service in some way—something that few applications can do easily at this time. A few application vendors, notably at the very top and bottom ends of the ERP market, are hooking up their applications to BSP services.

Exhibit 9.3 BSP Services for ERP Modules

Module	*Process*	*BSP Service*
System	FOREX management	Exchange rate download
General Ledger	Cash management	Bank statement download
Accounts Receivable	New customer acquisition	Credit checking
Accounts Payable	Invoice payment	Electronic funds transfer
Order Entry	Tax calculation	Sales tax look-up and calculation
Purchasing	Requisition processing	Reverse auction request for quote
Inventory	Reorder processing	Available to promise sourcing

For example, SAP is using its MySAP.com initiative to link users of its R/3 ERP suite to BSPs. Intuit is making use of its Internet gateway technology to hook users of its Quicken and QuickBooks accounting packages to BSPs.

Service portals, including Microsoft bCentral and many others, offer Web access to a range of BSP services from a single gateway Web page. The service portals effectively act as a broker for accessing BSP services, since users are typically just routed to the BSP's own Web site to take advantage of the service offering. Service portals are mushrooming—banks, utilities, and telecom providers offer them—but they depend on BSPs to offer value and suffer because they are not tightly linked with the in-house applications that can make best use of the service deliverable.

As the business Internet develops, the universe of BSPs will expand in terms of both breadth and depth. Managing a business process using a packaged application alone will no longer be competitive. Packaged software will have to be combined with Web services to truly take advantage of the Internet and benefit from the next phase of ongoing business process reengineering. Software as service may become the dominant paradigm and signal the end of the packaged application as we know it, much as electronic software distribution (ESD) over the Internet has destroyed the retail software store and its racks of shrink-wrapped offerings.

CHAPTER TEN

XML Everywhere

It looks certain, by the level of activity and analyst confirmation, that one of the most pervasive technologies in the world of e-business will be extensible markup language (XML). For this reason alone, a best practice for every e-business will be to understand how to leverage XML both within the business and in collaborations with business partners.

The scope of what XML can be used for is wide and includes as a:

- Document-level application programming interface
- Part of a B2B document exchange protocol
- Way to enable more efficient information searching
- Means to customize information viewing to personalize it for the recipient
- Facility to integrate data from heterogeneous sources

XML originated in standard generalized markup language (SGML). SGML became a standard of the International Organization for Standardization (ISO) back in 1986, and XML is a variant of SGML that came to life in 1998 as a version 1.0 specification from the World Wide Web Consortium (W3C). Since 1998 the interest in and development of XML-related products and services has been rapid, with a number of different types of XML-based document and document exchange "standards" being proposed by both technology vendors and users.

BEST PRACTICE ACTION ► STAY IN THE XML LOOP. Keep track of or participate in any XML initiatives in progress that relate to your industry sector or to those of your key business partners. The adoption of any sort of standard, especially for collaborative commerce, can leave businesses that have failed to keep up with standards initiatives out in the cold.

The following acronyms and terms are used in this chapter.

TERM	DESCRIPTION
API	Application programming interface
B2B	Business-to-business
DTD	Document type definition (see *schema*)
HTML	Hypertext markup language used for Web page layout and formatting
EDI	Electronic data interchange
Schema	Document that describes the structure and tags of an XML document
SGML	Standard generalized markup language
Shared context	A DTD or schema that explains the meaning of a set of XML tags
SOAP	Simple object access protocol
Tag	A label that describes the meaning of the data or how to format it
UDDI	Universal description, discovery, and integration
VAN	Value-added network used to route EDI traffic
VPN	Virtual private network on the Internet
W3C	World Wide Web Consortium
XBRL	Extensible business reporting language
XML	Extensible markup language used to create Web page metadata that describes content
XSL	Extensible style-sheet language used to format an XML document to view

UNDERSTANDING XML

XML vs. HTML

Hypertext markup language (HTML) is also a descendant of SGML but is focused on the formatting of data and its layout on a page—in other words, the visualizing of data.

Today, when you view a Web page in a browser, you are almost certainly looking at a HTML file. HTML uses a standard set of "tags," labels that describe the way your browser should render text and graphics. For example, the HTML tags <u> and </u> tell browsers to begin underlining and end underlining, respectively, so the HTML code <u>50.00</u> tells a Web browser to display the text as 50.00.

HTML provides a rich set of tags for data formatting and page layout, but its tags do not provide information about the meaning of the data. Suppose that you are viewing an invoice on a supplier's Web site and that the underlined 50.00 is in fact $50, the total amount due. While this fact may be clear to you when you view the invoice on screen, the HTML underlining tags do not indicate this important contextual data to a program that is trying "read" the invoice data to figure out what is owed.

XML improves on HTML by allowing tags that describe the data itself. In this sense, XML is a metadata language: metadata being data that describes data. The language does not use a standard set of tags; XML programmers define the tags they need when they create XML documents. Of course, this leads to confusion if there is no agreement over what a given set of tags mean. Thus some form of shared context is necessary to understand the content of an XML document.

Suppose that your supplier decides to make its invoices available online in XML rather than HTML. The programmer who creates the XML-based invoice document may make use of tags <type>, <currency>, and <total>, so that the document includes the code <type>invoice</type>, <currency>$</currency>, and <total>50.00</total>. If your accounting system understands the meaning of the <type>, <currency>, and <total> tags, it can read the XML document on the supplier's Web site and determine that the document is an invoice and that you owe $50. The shared context here is an understanding of what in fact the tags <type>,

<currency>, and <total> actually mean in the context of this particular XML invoice document.

Shared Context and Style Sheets

This shared context is described in a separate document called a document type definition (DTD) or schema, which describes the tags, their structure, and rules for usage. This schema lets humans and programs understand what individual data tags mean, explains their context and relationships (say as part of hierarchy tree), and lists any constraints (limitations) described by the tags on the use of that data. As a schema is a more extensive document definition structure than a DTD, I will use that term to refer to either structure.

An XML document without a schema is essentially useless to anyone other than the author, since no shared context exists to understand what it means. Business-application vendor and user consortia are developing or have released a wide range of XML schemas for use across many industry sectors. Once vendors and users reach a consensus on the schemas for common business documents such as invoices, purchase orders, and payments, the basis for a common e-business collaboration language will exist.

BEST PRACTICE ACTION ► **DEFINE YOUR DOCUMENTS.** Start an initiative to define the range of business documents used in your organization to determine which are likely to be covered by schemas being proposed by external bodies and which are internal to your organization. The latter type may demand their own "custom" schemas that may be made available only to internal staff and specific trusted business partners.

A shared context schema may be private or public. By making the schema public, you are exposing it to others so they know how to interface with your organization. These public shared context schemas are often stored in third-party repositories (i.e., an .ORG site, like Microsoft's BizTalk.org on the Web). Potential partners who want to understand the schemas in order to use them to collaborate with a business can view or download these schemas.

BEST PRACTICE ACTION ➤ **PROMOTE YOUR SCHEMAS.** Publish schemas for public viewing that will help attract potential business partners to collaborate with you electronically. Doing so may result in feedback on your schema design and inquiries from other businesses that want to collaborate with you using it.

In fact, as Exhibit 10.1 shows, an XML document may have at least two additional resources attached to it, a schema and one or more extensible style-sheet language (XSL) style sheets. A style sheet is a document that specifies what data to display and how to display it from the source XML document when viewed by a particular user or device type. For example, an XML invoice document may have three style sheets associated with it to determine how the invoice is displayed to:

- The supplier's internal staff on an intranet Web site
- The staff of the supplier's customers on an extranet Web site
- A device such as a wireless application protocol (WAP) phone

Exhibit 10.1 Three Types of XML Documents

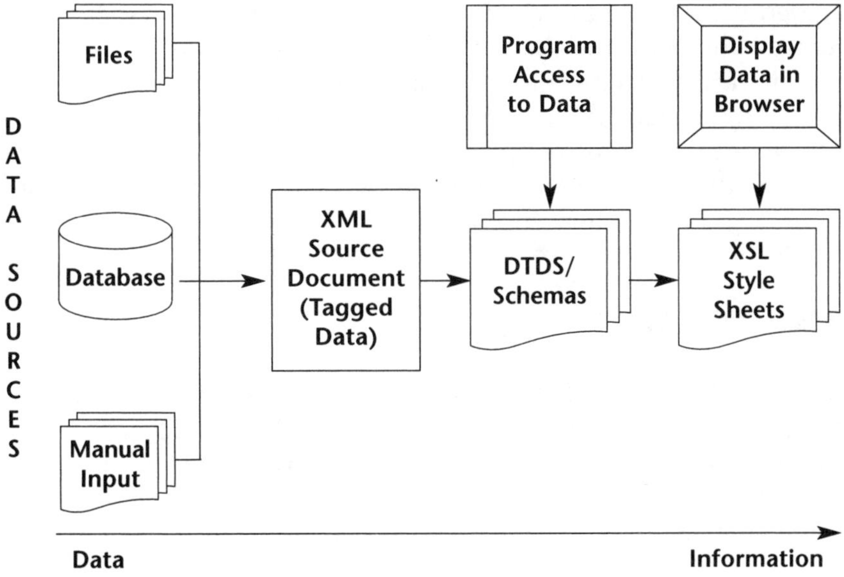

Today more and more Web sites are rejecting the use of HTML pages as the primary content structure and are moving toward dynamic and data-driven sites where

- The bulk of the content is stored in a database
- Content is extracted on demand from the database and assembled into an XML document
- A style sheet is then applied to the document, its selection depending on the user requesting the content and/or the device hosting the Web browser
- The content is formatted and presented to the user

This separation of data and structure from presentation is a major advantage of XML over HTML when it comes to content management of a Web site.

Using XML source documents and agreed-on shared context schemas, companies running different accounting and business management applications will be able to exchange documents and participate in cross-system, cross-organizational work flow. For example, a customer's enterprise resource planning (ERP) system might output a purchase order as an XML document and send the file across the Internet to a vendor's ERP system. Then, using an agreed-on schema, the vendor's ERP system might parse (i.e., interpret) the XML file that contains the purchase order data and automatically post the data as a sales order transaction in the vendor's ERP system. As a result, the transaction has become paperless and an issue-to-receipt order work flow fully automated to support the needs of such demanding business practices as just-in-time (JIT) inventory supply.

XML AND EDI

XML has the potential to become a universal data-description language, something that traditional electronic data interchange (EDI) standards (i.e., EDIFACT and X.12) failed to achieve because their high cost and complexity prevented many small businesses from using them. XML-based EDI does not depend on the need to install expensive EDI software nor does it require subscribing to supplier-controlled value-added networks (VANs).

Instead, XML-based EDI uses XML documents output directly from ERP systems, collaboration servers (see Chapter 3), and virtual private networks (VPNs) over the Internet as the means to transport documents between business partners. It remains to be seen whether the development of low-cost or free VPNs over the Internet will overcome the high-security and high-availability advantages of traditional subscription-based EDI VANs.

In any case, EDI-to-XML and XML-to-EDI translation is already taking place, so traditional EDI applications can continue to function in the world of XML. After the commonly used EDI transaction formats have been mapped to new XML schemas, EDI-based e-commerce will likely simply morph into XML-based e-commerce. Apart from EDI, other proprietary transaction exchange protocols, such as Open Financial Exchange (OFX) used to support online consumer banking, also are being converted to become XML-based.

> **BEST PRACTICE ACTION** ► **SKIP EDI—GO TO XML.** If you are not already using EDI in your organization, consider, XML-based alternatives. Check with your ERP vendor to understand what its strategy or deliverable is for XML-based B2B document exchange.

XML AS DOCUMENT API

XML performs a very useful function as a document application programming interface (API). By describing the data content of a document and its context, XML makes every document a standalone data source that can be mined for a variety of information and purposes.

Specific data within a document can be identified (through the schema), and the document can be "asset-stripped" by programs looking for specific data. That data then can be provided as is or aggregated with other data from other documents to create a new information view based on data culled from multiple sources.

Because data such as numeric values can be easily identified within an XML document, these values can be grabbed for aggregation purposes or to download into local spreadsheets for further analysis, or they can be tested against business rules to look for exceptions in the document data programmatically. XML-based financial reports open up the possibility for report mining engines to search across company reports looking for exception conditions that they can communicate via e-mail alerts or to combine data from multiple reports to create consolidation statements that they can deliver to information consumers via the Web.

XML tags can be used to describe the document itself, making the document easier for humans to understand, facilitating document management, and making it easier to search for and categorize the document in or across Web sites. New-generation XML-aware search engines are poised to take advantage of the growing number of XML documents and schemas already found on the Web.

XML tags can be used to define the work-flow characteristics or lifecycle of a document, such as an order or invoice. This can lead to automated supply chains where a document itself can manage its own work flow subject to business rules encoded in the document schema.

XML AND BUSINESS PROCESS REENGINEERING

XML is not just a replacement for traditional EDI and a useful document API. XML already has the ability and potential to reengineer a wide range of business processes, including:

- Procurement
- Financial reporting
- Using Web services

Procurement

One area in which XML can help businesses is in procurement. Use of a standard XML schema to describe items on offer in their online catalogs by Web storefronts, supplier communities, and e-auction sites would enable e-procurement systems that understand that schema to search the sites for particular items or suppliers.

For example, the e-procurement applications might look for sites with a <site type> tag of "e-auction"; then, within each auction site, they might find all items labeled with a certain XML identifier, such as <SKU>12345</SKU>, that are priced below <bid>$100</bid>. If an e-procurement application found the item it was looking for in multiple auctions, it could allow the user to comparison-shop to get the best deal in terms of price, quality, and delivery.

Using XML documents and schemas in this way has the potential to dramatically change the purchasing process. In effect, each requisition could be sent programmatically to a worldwide community of Web sites to return the best deals electronically for review by the requisitioner or a purchasing manager. All of this could be achieved in a time frame that few, if any, purchasing staff could match.

Financial Reporting

The American Institute of Chartered Public Accounts (AICPA) is working on an initiative with software vendors, Big Five accounting firms, and other bodies to define a standard "language" for financial reporting that they have dubbed XBRL (extensible business reporting language).

The idea of XBRL is to define a standard set of XML tags and schemas for describing reports. Doing so in effect creates a "report API." Reports output from one application could be read by any other application capable of parsing an XML document and with access to the appropriate XBRL schema.

Exhibit 10.2 shows how a single XML-based financial statement could collect data from multiple sources, provide data to dependent reports, and link to other relevant information sources. Besides reporting transaction data from an ERP system, data also could be collected from other XML documents, such as competitor financial statements or independent benchmark data, located on the Web. The XML document could embed URL hyperlinks to provide online access to other backup documents, such as auditor

Exhibit 10.2 XML Report

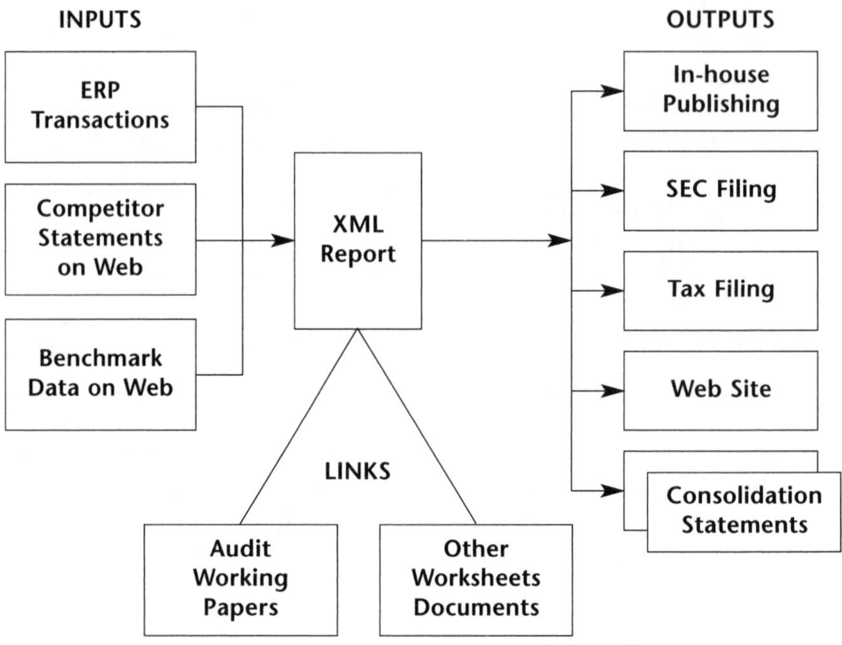

working papers or documents created in desktop spreadsheet or word processing applications. The XML document could be published to a printer or other file formats, or as a data provider for other XML reports used to file Securities and Exchange Commission reports or tax returns, deliver Web site content, or generate corporate consolidation statements.

Using XML tags to describe report content also makes it easy to:

- Expand and collapse reports visually based on the tag hierarchy
- Drill down from summary to detailed reports using special reference tags or hyperlinks to supporting report documents in HTML or XML formats
- Secure parts of the report content from prying eyes based on tag-level security
- Interrogate, or "asset-strip," reports for information by looking for certain tags

XML reports also will change the way that consolidations are processed. Once a subsidiary's financial statements are published to a corporate intranet in XML format, they can be mined programmatically for the numbers required to build higher-level consolidation statements. Much of the cumbersome report submission process that many larger corporations go through today to manage consolidations will disappear since the first-cut consolidation will be accomplished largely without human intervention.

BEST PRACTICE ACTION ► **REENGINEER REPORTING.** Think about the range of reports produced by your organization. How could standardizing on XML-based formats help reengineer processes such as consolidation, intercompany transaction processing, and exception discovery, and notification.

Finding and Using Web Services

As more software is delivered as a service over the Internet, XML will play an important role in finding and using these Web services. For example, XML-based directories of services located on the Web will make it easier to find potential service providers around the world. By publishing the schemas associated with those services, providers can make it easier for businesses to connect to the service, make service requests, and receive the service deliverable.

Recently a coalition of over 35 companies announced support for a new initiative called Universal Description, Discovery and Integration (UDDI). IBM and Microsoft have separately announced a new Web Services Description Language (WSDL).

UDDI will create a database of business information accessible via the Internet detailing the who, what, and how of Web services. Businesses can register in the database (who), describe the range of services they can deliver over the Internet (what), and help potential business partners understand how to connect to and use their service offering (how).

UDDI makes it easier to navigate the world of Web services, locate prospective business partners, and integrate applications or services with theirs. One area that will benefit greatly from UDDI is supply chain management via the Internet; through UDDI, the assembly of virtual supply chains will become a lot easier. Eventually UDDI may be able to partially or wholly automate finding and connecting to services programmatically, something that the development of WSDL will assist in.

WSDL is an XML syntax based both on IBM's Network Accessible Services Specification Language and Microsoft's SOAP (Simple Object Access Protocol) used to control access to messages or documents. If service providers use WSDL to help service consumers to request their service or respond with a service deliverable, the whole concept of loosely coupled applications (combinations of packaged applications and Web services) will become a reality.

BEST PRACTICE ACTION ► **USE UDDI.** Register your business and any services you can provide over the Internet in Web-based directories such as UDDI to make yourself known to communities of potential business partners.

The bottom line is that XML looks set to become a pervasive e-business technology, which means that XML skills will be in demand. Probably the most important best practice action to take from this chapter is to start developing or acquiring XML skills now so that your organization does not get caught short when XML really takes off.

CHAPTER ELEVEN

Hackett Benchmarking Solutions on Best Practices

Hackett Benchmarking| solutions (Hackett), part of AnswerThink Consulting Group, is recognized as a leader in collecting and analyzing data on business efficiency and effectiveness. Since 1988 Hackett has been collecting best practice benchmarking data. While the firm is just beginning to tackle benchmarking and best practices specifically related to e-businesses, much of the benchmarking data summarized in this chapter is useful to any type of business.

The chapter uses the year 2000 editions of Hackett's *Book of Numbers* as the primary source for best practice summaries covering

- Finance
- Human resources
- Information technology
- Planning and performance management
- Procurement

The data in this edition is based on 1999 surveys of some 1,400 businesses worldwide, a survey community that Hackett claims includes two-thirds of the Fortune 100 and one-third of the Fortune 500 companies. Prior data comparisons cited are usually to the last major Hackett survey, run in 1996.

HACKETT ON FINANCE

Hackett collects cost, performance, and best practice data across 29 finance processes organized into three categories: (1) transaction processing, (2) control and risk management, and (3) decision support. The *2000 Hackett Benchmarking | solutions Book of Numbers for Finance* is used as the source for the following data. The data in this book represents feedback from companies ranging from between $21 million to $57 billion in annual sales and employing finance staffs of between seven to 6,000 people.

Cost as a Percent of Revenue

Hackett has found that "On average, it costs a company 1.15 percent of annual revenue to provide financial services to the organization." But Hackett also found that "costs have been cut nearly in half since 1988, when they were 2.2 percent of revenue." It anticipates "that the average cost of finance will soon drop to less than one percent of revenue," but there are signs that "the focus on driving costs in finance down has not necessarily translated into increased effectiveness or value creation."

Hackett reckons that the companies with lower finance costs have a number of common characteristics. Each has:

- Simplified finance processes and enhanced integration with the core business processes
- Consolidated routine transaction processing into shared-services centers in order to drive standardization and maximize scale economies
- Streamlined and integrated systems that eliminate duplicate data capture and facilitate reporting
- Leveraged efficient work-flow technology, yielding low transaction costs
- Balanced control policies with degrees of materiality
- Addressed reorganizational implications of operating in highly automated frameworks, such as shifted skill development toward professionals

- Established clear leadership and vision
- Aligned finance priorities and objectives with the company's strategic direction
- Committed to using performance metrics on an ongoing basis

Hackett identifies four main components to finance cost: (1) fully loaded labor (compensation and benefits), (2) outsourcing, (3) systems, and (4) other. Labor remains the largest cost component, accounting for 59 cents of every dollar spent on finance in 1999. Interestingly, between 1996 and 1999 systems cost has been decreasing and outsourcing cost increasing, which indicates some switching of costs between in-house and outsourced systems. However, between 1996 and 1999 costs have fallen more dramatically in service companies than in goods-producing companies—a drop of 36 percent versus 9 percent.

Finance Staffing

Hackett finds that "The typical finance organization has an average of 122 full-time equivalent (FTE) employees per billion dollars of revenue." That represents "a 20 percent drop from 1996 and a 27 percent drop from 1994." But companies in the fourth quartile of the Hackett benchmark "have about 2.5 times as many finance employees (275) as those in the first quartile (108)." Hackett finds that "The average cost per finance FTE is $94,000, up only 2.5 percent from 1996."

Significantly, the largest decline in the number of finance workers as a percentage drop "has been in the category of decision support (31 percent)." And apparently managers are spending less time on decision support, "just 16 percent, down from 18 percent in 1996." This finding indicates that the transformation of finance has not focused on diverting staff to more value-added work.

Systems Complexity

According to Hackett data, "The typical company has about 29 systems per billion dollars of revenue, with the age of the systems averaging 4.4 years." In 1996, system age averaged around six years. But "First quartile companies have about 16 systems per billion dollars of revenue and just one data center."

Best Practices

From its research, Hackett summarizes finance best practices to be:

- The use of shared services centers and work-flow technology
- The move to streamline and standardize systems
- Early adoption of e-business applications for electronic data interchange (EDI) and electronic funds transfer (EFT)
- Investment in staff training and development
- More focus of time and resources into decision-support functions

Profile of a World-Class Finance Organization

The *2000 Hackett Benchmarking | solutions Book of Numbers for Finance* concludes with the summary profile of a world-class finance organization shown in Exhibit 11.1.

Exhibit 11.1 Hackett Benchmarking Summary: Finance

	Average	*World Class*
Cost as a percent of revenue	1.15%	<0.53%
FTEs per $ billion of revenues	122	<95
Vendor invoices per FTE	16,021	127,059
Processing locations	>3	1
Systems per process	2–3	1
Managers' time allocated to decision support	16%	33%
Closing cycle time	5–8 days	<2 days

HACKETT ON HUMAN RESOURCES

Hackett collects cost, performance, and best practice data across 21 human resources (HR) processes organized into four categories: (1) administration, (2) risk management, (3) employee life cycle, and (4) decision support. The *2000 Hackett Benchmarking | solutions Book of Numbers for Human Resources* is used as the source for the following data. The data in this book represents feedback from companies ranging from between $200 million to $147 billion in annual sales and employing HR staffs of between 10 to 1,600 people.

Cost Per Employee

Hackett has found that "On average, it costs a company $1584 annually to provide HR services to each employee." It also has found that "While costs for other knowledge-worker functions are steadily dropping those for HR have remained flat overall." Hackett reckons that the companies with lower HR costs have a number of common characteristics. They have:

- Simplified and standardized their HR processes to reduce administrative complexity
- Installed integrated systems that enable easier access to information
- Developed employee self-service tools to enhance service to employees
- Relied more on HR generalists with broader professional experience
- Set HR priorities that are in alignment with the strategic initiatives of the corporation
- Embraced selective sourcing strategies that take advantage of cost savings offered by outsourcing only those processes that vendors can deliver more efficiently

Economies of scale reduces HR costs in larger organizations, partly because smaller companies cannot dilute the costs of regulatory and compliance activities across a large employee base. The need to deal with organized labor is probably a key factor in pushing up HR costs in goods-producing companies compared to service companies.

Comparing 1999 results with 1996, labor costs have increased and outsourcing costs have declined. Hackett believes this is because outsourcing has not proven especially effective. Therefore, companies have used a selective-sourcing strategy to combine in-house with outsourced systems.

Employee Base Supported per HR Full-Time Equivalent

Hackett has found that the employee base supported per HR FTE has dropped since 1996 and the number of HR managers has grown by 15 percent, reflecting a more strategic focus. The scope of the HR service-delivery model is also expanding. The increased value of HR to the organization is reflected in the average cost per HR FTE rising by 12 percent (from 1996) to $71,512.

Human Resources has more managers per employee than any other knowledge-worker function surveyed by Hackett; the average ratio is one to three. These managers and staff are spending more and most of their time, at 32 percent, in looking after the employee life cycle. Another significant best practice finding in first-quartile companies is that HR people "spend 40 percent less time solving administrative problems than at the average company and almost twice as much time on decision support."

Systems Complexity

According to Hackett data, "The typical billion-dollar organization has about 9 HR systems per 1,000 employees." Hackett also has noted that "Though the number of systems used has declined only slightly in recent years, the age of systems is about half of what it was in 1996."

Best Practices

From its research, Hackett summarizes HR best practices to be:

- The use of a single HR shared-services center

- More time spent in decision support
- Delivery of self-service access to information
- Increased investment in employee development in the face of low unemployment
- A recognition that HR has a strategic organizational function
- A commitment to selective sourcing rather than wholesale outsourcing of HR systems

Profile of a World-Class HR Organization

The *2000 Hackett Benchmarking | solutions Book of Numbers for Human Resources* concludes with the summary profile of a world-class HR organization shown in Exhibit 11.2.

Exhibit 11.2 Hackett Benchmarking Summary: HR

	Average	*World Class*
Cost per employee	$1,584	<$1,200
Labor cost per HR FTE	$71,512	<$57,000
Systems per 1,000 FTEs	8.7	1.4
Employees supported per FTE	72	313
Discrete records per FTE	5.5	1.0
Payroll cost per employee	$1.68	$0.27

HACKETT ON IT

Hackett collects cost, performance, and best practice data across 10 information technology (IT) processes organized into three categories: (1) operational support, (2) investment, and (3) decision support. The *2000 Hackett Benchmarking | solutions Book of Numbers for Information Technology* is used as the source for the following data. The data in this book represents feedback from companies ranging from between $30 million to $44 billion in annual sales and employing IT staffs of between 13 to 5,000 people.

Cost Per End User

Hackett has found that "On average, it costs a company $9,167 per end-user to provide IT services." But of this cost, the labor and outsourcing components have come down the most since 1996 and the systems cost component has increased by 13 percent, probably reflecting more spent on software.

Hackett reckons that the companies with lower IT costs have a number of common characteristics. They have:

- Simplified and standardized their operations to reduce complexity
- Designed a better span-of-control personnel mix
- Established clear leadership and vision
- Improved the effectiveness of project managers
- Aligned IT priorities with the company's strategic direction
- Delivered higher levels of customer service
- Proactively managed their supplier relationships
- Committed to using performance metrics on an ongoing basis

Hackett also points out that cost per end user is certain to be higher in businesses such as telecommunications and financial services because in these types of business, "IT does more than support the operations: It is the operations."

IT Staffing

Hackett finds that "The IT organization in the typical billion-dollar company supports 3,551 end-users, a jump of 27 percent from our previous benchmark." This increase is due to the "vastly increased technology requirements for employee populations." Some 93 percent of staff are considered managers; the span of control of these managers averages about one to nine across the IT organization.

Investment Projects

According to Hackett data, "the average company delivers almost half of large IT projects late and over budget . . . [and] companies with lower spending patterns consistently fail to deliver infrastructure development projects on-time and on-budget."

Hackett also has found that in 1999, "the client/server platform is utilized for almost half of the production applications, for the first time surpassing even mid-range usage." And "While the mainframe platform remains viable for companies that process large volumes of transactions, it accounts for only 7 percent of the number of production applications supported."

Software Development and End User Support

Hackett has found that "Investments in software development have clearly shifted towards applications that support revenue-generating functions." Packaged software now is more prevalent than custom-built software.

First-quartile companies have over 115 users per server, compared to 53 in the previous survey. User calls to help desks have doubled in recent years, which partly explains why the average cost of end user support has jumped 23 percent and the time allocation for end user support and training has increased 50 percent in recent years.

Best Practices

From its research, Hackett summarizes IT best practices to be:

- The use of standards to reduce system complexity and cost
- The use of selective sourcing to outsource only those processes that drive costs lower
- The availability of a mature yet flexible technology infrastructure
- Positioning the chief information officer and the IT organization as strategic enablers for the business

Profile of a World-Class IT Organization

The *2000 Hackett Benchmarking| solutions Book of Numbers for Information Technology* concludes with the summary profile of a world-class IT organization shown in Exhibit 11.3.

Exhibit 11.3 Hackett Benchmarking Summary: IT Organizations

	Average	*World Class*
Cost per end user	$9,167	$4,308
Age of applications (years)	3.7	2.4
Data centers/1,000 users	1.4	0.7
Project completion on time and on budget	64%	85%
Standards enforcement	69%	100%
Spans of control	1:9	1:16
Help desk calls/end user	10.4	5.0

HACKETT ON PLANNING AND PERFORMANCE MEASUREMENT

Hackett collects cost, performance, and best practice data across 13 planning and performance measurement (PPM) activities organized into four categories: (1) strategic planning, (2) tactical and financial planning, (3) performance reporting, and (4) analysis and forecasting. The *2000 Hackett Benchmarking| solutions Book of Numbers for Planning and Performance Measurement* is used as the source for the following data. The data in this book represents feedback from companies ranging from between $15 million to $150 billion in annual sales and employing staffs of between 200 to 600,000 people.

Cycle Time

Hackett has found that "For the typical company, planning takes up to nine months, with tactical and financial planning burning up five of these months" and "The average company also requires a minimum of nine days to close the books and report results."

This information has led Hackett to conclude that "The planning process is so slow at some companies that the work is out of date before it's even completed, rendering the exercise useless." Nevertheless: "Top performing companies have condensed planning to less than two months," and these companies also could close their books in two days.

Hackett reckons that the companies with lower PPM cycle times have a number of common characteristics. Each has:

- Set clear targets up to guide PPM plan development
- Fully integrated strategic and tactical plans that link measures to business goals and compensation
- A rolling forecast of only major business variables and uses exception-based reporting
- Limited detailed line items to those things that are truly material drivers of the business
- Stakeholder/market expectations and competitive indicators as the most important planning drivers
- A single, enterprise-wide planning and reporting system with common data definitions and online access

Level of Staff Effort

Hackett has found that "For every billion dollars in revenue, the average company invests more than 25,000 person-days annually in strategic, financial and tactical planning." Significantly, around one-third of that time is spent simply collecting and validating data. This, plus other activities, leaves only 20 percent of the planning effort left "for thinking about the future impact of the numbers on the business."

One reason for this limited effort is because the average company budgets some 230 line items, as opposed to 40 line items in first-quartile companies. Only 19 percent of companies utilize exception-based variances to focus in on what is material or volatile variance.

Technology Tools

According to Hackett data, the general ledger remains the key information source for most companies (with a data warehouse second), and "nearly 90 percent of companies depend either moderately or extensively on the close cycle for management information." This approach forces companies to spend large amounts of time gathering information and less time actually analyzing it.

Almost half the companies surveyed by Hackett used a balanced scorecard, but Hackett is "convinced that these tools have been only minimally beneficial for planning and performance measurement" because the scorecards

- Are not balanced, since 75 percent of the performance measures are financial in nature
- Focus on historical results, missing current or potential risks and opportunities

Best Practices

From its research, Hackett summarizes PPM best practices to be:

- The use of tightly integrated strategic, financial, and tactical plans
- Tying incentives to the achievement of key strategic objectives
- A "fearless forecasting" approach based on shorter time lines or material events
- Automation of the management reporting process through better use of new technology

Profile of a World-Class PPM Organization

The *2000 Hackett Benchmarking | solutions Book of Numbers for Planning and Performance Measurement* concludes with the summary profile of a world-class PPM organization shown in Exhibit 11.4.

HACKETT ON PROCUREMENT

Hackett collects cost, performance and best practice data across 15 procurement processes organized into three categories: (1) operational support, (2) control and risk management, and (3) decision support. The *2000 Hackett Benchmarking | solutions Book of Numbers for Procurement* is used as the source for the following data. The data in this book represents feedback from companies

Exhibit 11.4 Hackett Benchmarking Summary: PPM

	Average	*World Class*
Tactical and financial planning	4 months	1 month
Strategic planning	5 months	1 month
Level of budget detail (line items)	230	15
Planning and reporting resource requirement (person days per billion of revenue)	25,703	700
Percent of time spent on forecasting/Action planning	20%	44%
Forecasting basis	Current calendar year	Rolling quarterly

ranging from between $33 million to $27 billion in annual sales and employing procurement staffs of between six to 800 people.

Cost as a Percent of Purchased Costs

Hackett has found that "On average a company spends just under one percent of its purchased costs to manage the procurement function." But "the average cost of procurement has decreased only slightly in recent years, about 5 percent." However, average procurement cost as a percent of purchased costs varies widely—from 0.30 percent to 4.38 percent. The top 25 percent of companies surveyed have costs of between 0.3 percent and 0.83 percent, while the bottom 25 percent of companies surveyed have costs of between 2.01 and 4.38 percent.

Hackett reckons that the companies with lower procurement costs have a number of common characteristics:

- Automated procurement processes that allow for more efficient and effective day-to-day operations
- Reductions in the overall supplier base and the development of supplier performance measures
- Integrated systems that provide high-quality contract and price information across the enterprise

- Aggressive use of procurement cards for small-dollar purchases
- Online libraries (or catalogs) that allow purchasers to self-procure standard and commodity products

It can be harder for service companies to make their procurement processes as efficient as goods-producing companies. Goods-producing companies are more likely to have a greater volume of high-dollar, high-value purchases and are more likely to purchase a high number of standard items; these factors decrease the number of purchase orders and overall order complexity. Larger companies—those with over $1 billion in purchased costs—also have been able to keep their procurement costs nearly 50 percent lower than smaller companies, an advantage that is partly due to the fact that larger companies can afford to invest in new technology.

Procurement Staffing

Hackett finds that "Procurement staffs have an average of 137 full-time equivalent (FTE) employees per billion dollars of purchased costs. That represents a 13 percent decline and has largely been driven by productivity savings associated with technology investments." But as "the staff mix has shifted toward more buying specialists and fewer clerical workers," the average cost per procurement FTE has increased by 7 percent to about $76,000.

Significantly, some 72 percent of procurement's time is spent in lower value-added activities, such as requisition and purchase-order processing, supplier selection, and material receipts processing. Only 14 percent of time is spent on higher value-added decision support activities. The ratio of managers to staff averages about one to eight across the procurement organization, and Hackett has found "in general that there is a strong correlation between higher spans of control and world-class performance."

Systems Complexity

According to Hackett data, "The typical company has about 27 procurement systems per billion dollars of purchased costs, one of the largest numbers in the corporation. These systems tend to be highly customized and complex, and are typically not well integrated. The average age of these systems is over six years." Yet despite recent investments in enterprise resource planning systems, "the number and age of procurement systems have dropped only marginally over the last three years."

Best Practices

From its research, Hackett summarizes procurement best practices to be:

- The use of automated systems—including use of bar-coding technology and electronic data interchange for order placement, order release, order acknowledgment, and shipping notifications, among others
- The use of procurement cards—p-card use has more than quadrupled over the past three years to include 18 percent of purchasing transactions
- Improved supplier management including centralized contracting with suppliers and "more active involvement and partnering with suppliers"
- Transaction consolidation involving the use of blanket purchase orders and long-term supply contracts

Profile of a World-Class Procurement Organization

The *2000 Hackett Benchmarking | solutions Book of Numbers for Procurement* concludes with the summary profile of a world-class procurement organization shown in Exhibit 11.5.

HACKETT ON E-BUSINESS

Hackett has only recently begun to survey businesses on specific issues related to e-business. Its recent (1999–2000) research in this area is based on responses from companies averaging $15 billion in annual revenues and ranging in size from $50 million to more

EXHIBIT 11.5 Hackett Benchmarking Summary: Procurement

	Average	*World Class*
Cost as a percent of purchased costs	1%	<0.67%
FTEs per $ billion of purchased costs	137	88
Suppliers with 90% of purchased costs	1,857	433
POs handled per FTE	5,027	13,163
Percent processed electronically	43%	73%
Procurement card usage	18%	41%

than $50 billion in revenue per year. Results from this research indicate that:

- Companies are budgeting for a 68 percent increase in e-business investment during the next two years, and some 40 percent of companies report that improving customer relations would be the primary driver for this investment.
- Most companies are not reviewing their e-business plans at least every three months, and some are struggling to review their plans annually.
- The typical company in the study expects its procurement function to receive the greatest amount of e-business investment.
- The typical company in the study expects Web-enabled benefits administration activity to increase by 35 percent, recruiting via the Internet to increase by 30 percent, and Web-based e-learning to increase by as much as 60 percent.

Hackett research also indicates that poor systems integration is holding back improvements in supply-chain management. For example, of the companies surveyed:

- 40 percent said they had yet to integrate their supply chains with other e-business systems

- 73 percent said they had not changed their traditional shipping methods
- 55 percent said they have yet to eliminate any fulfillment processes

Many of Hackett's findings indicate that much of the technology discussed in this book needs to be implemented to move businesses not just to best-practice e-business but also to e-business period.

SELECTED READINGS

E-BUSINESS BOOKS

TITLE	AUTHOR	PUBLISHED BY
eBusiness Essentials	Mark Norris, Steve West, Kevin Gaughan	John Wiley & Sons, 2000
E-Business: Roadmap for Success	Ravi Kalakota, Marcia Robinson	Addison-Wesley, 1999
Enterprise Application Integration	David S. Linthicum	Addison-Wesley, 2000
Internet Standards and Protocols	Dilip C. Naik	Microsoft Press, 1998
Killer Content Strategies for Web Content and E-Commerce	Mai-lan Tomsen	Addison-Wesley, 2000
Managing Knowledge: A Practical Web-based Approach	Wayne Applehans, Alden Globe, Greg Laugero	Addison-Wesley, 1999
Net Success: 24 Leaders in Web Commerce Show You How to Put the Internet to Work for Your Business	Christina Ford Haylock, Len Muscarella, with Ron Schultz (eds.)	Adams Media, 1999
Understanding Electronic Commerce	David Kosiur	Microsoft Press, 1997
XML: A Manager's Guide	Kevin Dick	Addison-Wesley, 2000

E-BUSINESS MAGAZINES

TITLE	WEB SITE
Business 2.0	business20.com
Business Finance	businessfinancemag.com
eCompanyNow	ecompany.com
ERP News	erpnews.com
Fast Company	fastcompany.com
The Industry Standard	thestandard.com
Intelligent Enterprise	intelligenterprise.com
Strategy & Business	strategy-business.com
Technology Review	techreview.com

E-BUSINESS AND VENDOR WEB SITES BY CHAPTER

CHAPTER		VENDOR	WEB SITE
2	**E-Business Management: Going Beyond ERP**	CMP Outsourcing ERP SAP	Intelligenterp.com Outsourcingerp.com mysap.com
3	**Monitor to Manage: Enterprise Positioning System**	Business Intelligence Cognos Searchspace	OLAPreport.com Cognos.com Searchspace.com
4	**Collaborate to Compete**	CMP NetMarketMakers RosettaNet WebMethods	IntelligentEAI.com Netmarketmakers.com RosettaNet.org Webmethods.com

CHAPTER	VENDOR	WEB SITE *(continued)*
5 **Customer Relationship Management**	CMP	IntelligentCRM.com
	Seibel Systems	Siebel.com
6 **E-Procurement**	Ariba	Ariba.com
	CommerceOne	Commerceone.com
	Mondus	Mondus.com
	Open Buying on Internet	Openbuy.org
	Works	Works.com
7 **Knowledge Management**	CMP	IntelligentKM.com
8 **Digital Asset Management**	Content Technologies	Contenttechnologies.com
	Plumtree	Plumtree.com
	Viador	Viador.com
9 **Software as Service**	All About ASP	Allaboutasp.org
	ASP Industry Consortium	Aspindustry.org
	ASP Street	Aspstreet.com
	Bowstreet Software	Bowstreet.com
	BusinessTechnology	Businesstechnology.com
	Cfoinfo	Cfoinfo.com
10 **XML Everywhere**	Microsoft BizTalk	Biztalk.org
	World Wide Web Consortium	W3c.org
	XBRL	Xbrl.org
11 **Hackett Benchmarking Solutions on Best Practices**	AnswerThink	Answerthink.com

GLOSSARY

Alert	Electronic notification to inform a person that an event has occurred
Analytic software	Software used to analyze data and convert it into information
API	Application programming interface
ASP	Application service provider
B2B	Business to business
B2C	Business to consumer
BI	Business intelligence
BSP	Business service provider on the Internet
Bureau	Third party that maintains host computers for time-sharing use
Cart	Shopping cart that represents an order placed on a Web store
Catalog	Item catalog hosted on a Web server for online browsing and buying
Clickstream	Series of mouse-clicks used to navigate a Web page or Web site
Community	Group of suppliers and/or customers using a trading hub
Consumer	Individual customer paying by cash or credit/debit card
Content	Documents, reports, news feeds, graphics, and the like viewed on Web sites
Context warehouse	Database of transaction data used by contextual monitoring software
CRM	Customer relationship management

Data mart	Subset of a data warehouse focused on a specific business domain
Data source	File system or database where data is stored and accessed from
Data warehouse	Database of aggregated information used by analytic software
Domain	Area of expertise relevant to knowledge management
Domain expert	Person or Web site with expertise relating to a specific domain
DTD	Document type definition (see *schema*)
EBPP	Electronic bill presentment and payment
eCRM	E-customer relationship management
E-customer	Customer who interacts primarily electronically with a supplier
EDI	Electronic data interchange
EDIFACT	Standard used for defining EDI documents or transactions
EDM	Electronic document management
EFT	Electronic funds transfer
EIS	Executive information system
E-learning	Distance learning over the Internet
E-procurement	Paperless process for buying goods and services from suppliers via the Internet
EPS	Enterprise positioning system
ERP	Enterprise resource planning
Event	Condition that managers determine is noteworthy to the business
Exception	Event considered to be exceptional for the business activity
Firewall	Software to protect systems from unauthorized access via the Internet
Fulfillment	Process of delivering a product or service to a customer

HTML	Hypertext markup language used for Web page layout and formatting
Hub	Web site that acts as the matchmaker between buyers and sellers
Interaction channel	Means of communicating with a customer electronically
IP (address)	Internet protocol address—a specific node on the Internet
ISP	Internet service provider
KM	Knowledge management
KPI	Key performance indicator
Maverick buying	Buying nonrecommended products from nonpreferred suppliers
MRO	Maintenance, repairs, and operations
MRP	Manufacturing resource planning
OBI	Open buying on the Internet (document exchange standards)
Order (PO)	Order placed with a supplier to deliver a product or service
ORM	Operational resource management
Outcome	Result of applying rules to an event occurrence
Outsourcing	Running business processes or functions at third-party technology sites
P-card	Purchasing card used to consolidate low-value, high-volume purchases
Personalization	Customizing a deliverable to the needs of an individual
Portal	Web-based gateway to people, processes, systems, and content
Portlet	Discrete "applet" that delivers functions and/or content within a portal
Preferred supplier	Supplier with whom special buying terms have been negotiated
Reportal	Web-based report organization and viewing software

Request/response	Work flow between service user and service provider
Requisition (PR)	Request from an employee to purchase a product or service
RFB	Request for bid (sent to a reverse auction hub)
RFO	Request for offer (sent to a conventional auction hub)
ROI	Return on investment
RTB	Response to bid (returned from an auction or hub site)
Rule	Business logic applied to an event to determine its outcome
Schema	Document that describes the structure and tags of an XML document
Scorecard	Visual representation of key business metrics and their current status
Self-service	Providing the means for customers to serve themselves via the Internet
SFA	Sales force automation
SGML	Standard generalized markup language
Shared context	DTD or schema that explains the meaning of a set of XML tags
Shared services	Consolidating processing at a specific "service center" site
SLA	Service-level agreement (with ASP, BSP, ISP)
Subscriber	Individual who needs to be informed that an event has occurred
Subscription	Fee paid to subscribe to a service over a period of time
Tag	Label that describes the meaning of the data or how to format it
TCO	Total cost of ownership
Teamware	Software focused on supporting collaborative activities over the Internet

Three-way match	Matching the order (1) to the receipt (2) to the invoice (3)
Time-sharing	Sharing the power of a host processor with other businesses
Trading hub	Web site for connecting buyers and sellers for online trading (a.k.a. exchange)
UDDI	Universal description, discovery, and integration
VAN	Value-added network—used to route EDI traffic between business partners
VPN	Virtual private network—connects two points across the Internet
W3C	World Wide Web Consortium
Warehouse	Database storing a collection of aggregated and/or categorized data
Web store	Online storefront accessible over the Internet
X.12	Standard used for defining EDI documents or transactions
XBRL	Extensible business reporting language
XML	Extensible markup language used to create Web page metadata
XSL	Extensible style-sheet language used to format XML document for viewing

INDEX